ISBN 978-1-330-48671-9
PIBN 10068263

1 MONTH OF
FREE
READING

at

www.ForgottenBooks.com

By purchasing this book you are eligible for one month membership to ForgottenBooks.com, giving you unlimited access to our entire collection of over 700,000 titles via our web site and mobile apps.

To claim your free month visit:

www.forgottenbooks.com/free68263

Similar Books Are Available from
www.forgottenbooks.com

ADVICE

TO THE

PRIVILEGED ORDERS

IN THE

SEVERAL STATES OF EUROPE,

RESULTING FROM THE

NECESSITY AND PROPRIETY

OF

A GENERAL REVOLUTION IN THE PRINCIPLE OF GOVERNMENT.

PART I.

LONDON:

PRINTED FOR J. JOHNSON, IN ST. PAUL'S CHURCH-YARD,

ADVERTISEMENT.

SPEEDILY will be publifhed the fecond part of this work; in which will be treated the four laft fubjects mentioned in the plan, as explained in the Introduction : viz. *Revenue and Public Expenditure, Means of Subfiftence, Literature, Sciences and Arts, War and Peace.*

ERRATUM.

Page 8, line 2 from bottom, for *or* read *of.* -

ADVICE

PRIVILEGED ORDERS.

INTRODUCTION.

THE French Revolution is at laft not only ac-
complifhed, but its accomplifhment univerfally acknowledged, beyond contradiction abroad,
or the power of retraction at home. It has finifh-
ed its work, by organizing a government, on principles approved by reafon; an object long con-
templated by different writers, but never before
exhibited, in this quarter of the globe. The experiment now in operation will folve a queftion of
the firft magnitude in human affairs: Whether
Theory and *Practice*, which always agree together
in things of flighter moment, are really to remain
eternal enemies in the higheft concerns of men?

B   The

The change of government in France is, properly fpeaking, a renovation of fociety; an object peculiarly fitted to hurry the mind into a field of thought, which can fcarcely be limited by the concerns of a nation, or the improvements of an age. As there is a tendency in human nature to imitation; and, as all the apparent caufes exift in moft of the governments of the world, to induce the people to wifh for a fimilar change, it becomes interefting to the caufe of humanity, to take a deliberate view of the real nature and extent of this change, and find what are the advantages and difadvantages to be expected from it.

There is not that necromancy in politics, which prevents our forefeeing, with tolerable certainty, what is to be the refult of operations fo univerfal, in which all the people concur. Many truths are as perceptible when firft prefented to the mind, as an age or a world of experience could make them; others require only an indirect and collateral experience; fome demand an experience direct and pofitive.

It

It is happy for human nature, that in morals we have much to do with this firſt claſs of truths, leſs with the ſecond, and very little with the third; while in phyſics we are perpetually driven to the ſlow proceſs of patient and poſitive experience.

The Revolution in France certainly comes recommended to us under one aſpect which renders it at firſt view extremely inviting: it is the work of argument and rational conviction, and not of the ſword. The *ultima ratio regum* had nothing to do with it. It was an operation deſigned for the benefit of the people; it originated in the people, and was conducted by the people. It had therefore a legitimate origin; and this circumſtance entitles it to our ſerious contemplation, on two accounts: becauſe there is ſomething venerable in the idea, and becauſe other nations, in ſimilar circumſtances, will certainly be diſpoſed to imitate it.

I ſhall therefore examine the nature and conſequences of a ſimilar revolution in government, as it will affect the following principal objects, which

make

make up the affairs of nations in the prefent ftate
of Europe :

I. The feudal Syftem,

II. The Church,

III. The Military,

IV. The Adminiftration of Juftice,

V. Revenue and public Expenditure,

VI. The Means of Subfiftence,

VII. Literature, Sciences and Arts,

VIII. War and Peace.

The interefts of kings and hereditary fucceffion
will not be forgotten in this arrangement; they
will be treated with the privileged orders under
the feveral heads to which their different claims
belong.

It muft be of vaft importance to all the claffes
of fociety, as it now ftands claffed in Europe, to
calculate

calculate before hand what they are to gain or to lofe by the approaching change; that, like prudent ftock-jobbers, they may buy in or fell out, according as this great event fhall affect them.

Philofophers and contemplative men, who may think themfelves difinterefted fpectators of fo great a political drama, will do well to confider how far the cataftrophe is to be beneficial or detrimental to the human race; in order to determine whether in confcience they ought to promote or difcourage, accelerate or retard it, by the publication of their opinions. It is true, the work was fet on foot by this fort of men; but they have not all been of the fame opinion relative to the beft organization of the governing power, nor how far the reform of abufes ought to extend. Montefquieu, Voltaire, and many other refpectable authorities, have accredited the principle, that republicanifm is not convenient for a great ftate. Rouffeau and others take no notice of the diftinction between great and fmall ftates, in deciding, that this is the only government proper to enfure the happinefs, and fupport the dignity of man. Of the former opinion

B 3

was

was a great majority of the conftituting national affembly of France. Probably not many years will pafs, before a third opinion will be univerfally adopted, never to be laid afide: That the republican principle is not only proper and fafe for the government of any people; but, that its propriety and fafety are in proportion to the magnitude of the fociety and the extent of the territory.

Among fincere enquirers after truth, all general queftions on this fubject reduce themfelves to this: Whether men are to perform their duties by an eafy choice or an expenfive cheat; or, whether our reafon be given us to be improved or ftifled, to render us greater or lefs than brutes, to increafe our happinefs or aggravate our mifery.

Among thofe whofe anxieties arife only from intereft, the enquiry is, how their privileges or their profeffions are to be affected by the new order of things. Thefe form a clafs of men refpectable both for their numbers and their fenfibility; it is our duty to attend to their cafe. I fincerely hope to adminifter fome confolation to them in the

courfe

course of this essay. And though I have a better opinion of their philanthropy, than political opponents generally entertain of each other, yet I do not altogether rely upon their presumed sympathy with their fellow-citizens, and their supposed willingness to sacrifice to the public good ; but I hope to convince them, that the establishment of general liberty will be less injurious to those who now live by abuses, than is commonly imagined ; that protected industry will produce effects far more astonishing than have ever been calculated ; that the increase of enjoyments will be such, as to ameliorate the condition of every human creature.

To persuade this class of mankind that it is neither their duty nor their interest to endeavour to perpetuate the ancient forms of government, would be a high and holy office ; it would be the greatest act of charity to them, as it might teach them to avoid a danger that is otherwise unavoidable ; it would preclude the occasion of the people's indulging what is sometimes called a ferocious disposition, which is apt to grow upon the revenge of injuries, and render them less harmonious in their

new

new ſtation of citizens; it would prevent the civil wars, which might attend the inſurrections of the people, where there ſhould be a great want of unanimity,—for we are not to expect in every country that mildneſs and dignity which have uniformly characterized the French, even in their moſt tumultuous movements *: it would remove every obſtacle

* Whatever reaſon may be given for the fact, I believe all thoſe who have been witneſſes of what are called *mobs* in France (during the revolution) will join with me in opinion, that they were by no means to be compared with Engliſh mobs, in point of indiſcriminate ferocity and private plunder. A popular commotion in Paris was uniformly directed to a certain well-explained object; from which it never was known to deviate. Whether this object were to hang a man, to arreſt the king, to intimidate the court, or to break the furniture of a hotel, all other perſons and all other property, that fell in the way of the mob, were perfectly ſafe.

The truth is, thoſe collections were compoſed of honeſt and induſtrious people, who had nothing in view but the public good. They believed that the cauſe of their country required an execution of juſtice more prompt than could be expected from any eſtabliſhed tribunal. Beſides, they were in the criſis of a revolution, when they were ſenſible, that the crimes or their enemies would remain unpuniſhed, for want of a known rule

obftacle and every danger that may feem to attend that rational fyftem of public felicity to which the nations of Europe are moving with rapid ftrides, and which in profpect is fo confoling to the enlightened friends of humanity,

To induce the men who now govern the world to adopt thefe ideas, is the duty of thofe who now poffefs them. I confefs the tafk at firft view appears more than Herculean ; it will be thought an object from which the eloquence of the clofet muft fhrink in defpair, and which prudence would leave to the more powerful argument of events. But I believe at the fame time that fome fuccefs may be expected; that though the harveft be great, the

rule by which they could be judged. Though a violation of *right*, is not always a violation of *law*; yet, in their opinion, occafions might exift, when it would be dangerous to let it pafs with impunity.

It is indeed to be hoped, that, whenever mobs in other countries fhall be animated by the fame caufe, they will conduct themfelves with the fame dignity; and that this fingular phenomenon will be found not altogether attributable to national character.

laborers

laborers may not be few; that prejudice and intereſt cannot always be relied on to garriſon the mind againſt the aſſaults of truth. This belief, ill-grounded as it may appear, is ſufficient to animate me in the cauſe; and to the venerable hoſt of re-publican wiiters, who have preceded me in the diſcuſſions occaſioned by the French revolution, this belief is my only apology for offering to join the fraternity, and for thus practically declaring my opinion, that they have not exhauſted the ſubject.

Two very powerful weapons, the force of reaſon and the force of numbers, are in the hands of the political reformers. While the uſe of the firſt brings into action the ſecond, and enſures its co-operation, it remains a ſacred duty, impoſed on them by the God of reaſon, to wield with dexterity this mild and beneficent weapon, before recurring to the uſe of the other; which, though legitimate, may be leſs harmleſs; though infallible in operation, may be leſs glorious in victory.

Tho

The tyrannies of the world, whatever be the appellation of the government under which they are exercifed, are all ariftocratical tyrannies. An ordinance to plunder and murder, whether it fulminate from the Vatican, or fteal filently forth from the Harem; whether it come clothed in the *certain fcience* of a Bed of Juftice, or in the legal folemnities of a bench of lawyers; whether it be purchafed by the careffes of a woman, or the treafures of a nation,——never confines its effects to the benefit of a fingle individual; it goes to enrich the whole combination of confpirators, whofe bufinefs it is to dupe and to govern the nation. It carries its own bribery with itfelf through all its progrefs and connexions,——in its origination, in its enaction, in its vindication, in its execution; it is a fertilizing ftream, that waters and vivifies its happy plants in the numerous channels of its communication. Minifters and fecretaries, commanders of armies, contractors, collectors and tide-waiters, intendants, judges and lawyers,——whoever is permitted to drink of the falutary ftream,——are all interefted in removing the obftructions and in praifing the fountain from whence it flows.

The

The ſtate of human nature requires that this ſhould be the caſe. Among beings ſo nearly equal in power and capacity as men of the ſame community are, it is impoſſible that a ſolitary tyrant ſhould exiſt. Laws that are deſigned to operate unequally on ſociety, muſt offer an excluſive intereſt to a conſiderable portion of its members, to enſure their execution upon the reſt. Hence has ariſen the neceſſity of that ſtrange complication in the governing power, which has made of politics an inexplicable ſcience; hence the reaſon for arming one claſs of our fellow-creatures with the weapons of bodily deſtruction, and another with the myſterious artillery of the vengeance of heaven; hence the cauſe of what in England is called the independence of the judges, and what on the continent has created a judiciary nobility, a ſet of men who purchaſe the privilege of being the profeſſional enemies of the people, of ſelling their deciſions to the rich, and of diſtributing individual oppreſſion; hence the ſource of thoſe Draconian codes of criminal juriſprudence which enſhrine the idol Property in a bloody ſanctuary, and teach the modern European, that his life is of leſs value than

the

the fhoes on his feet; hence the positive difcouragements laid upon agriculture, manufactures, commerce, and every method of improving the condition of men; for it is to be obferved, that in every country the fhackles impofed upon induftry are in proportion to the degree of general defpotifm that reigns in the government. This arifes not only from the greater debility and want of enterprife in the people, but from the fuperior neceffity that fuch governments are under, to prevent their fubjects from acquiring that eafe and information, by which they could difcern the evil and apply the remedy.

To the fame fruitful fource of calamities we are to trace that perverfity of reafon, which, in governments where men are permitted to difcufs political fubjects, has given rife to thofe perpetual fhifts of fophiftry by which they vindicate the prerogative of kings. In one age it is the *right of conqueft*, in another *the divine right*, then it comes to be a *compact between king and people*, and laft of all, it is faid to be founded on general convenience, *the good of the whole community*. In England

land

land thefe feveral arguments have all had their day; though it is aftonifhing that the two former could ever have been the fubjects of rational debate: the firft is the logic of the mufquet, and the fecond of the chalice; the one was buried at Rennimede on the fignature of Magna Charta, the other took its flight to the continent with James the Second. The compact of king and people has lain dormant the greater part of the prefent century; till it was roufed from flumber by the French revolution, and came into the fervice of Mr. Burke.

Hafty men difcover their errors when it is too late. It had certainly been much more confiftent with the temperament of that writer's mind, and quite as ferviceable to his caufe, to have recalled the fugitive claim of the divine right of kings. It would have given a myftic force to his declama-tion, afforded him many new epithets, and fur-nifhed fubjects perfectly accordant with the copious charges of *facrilege, atheifm, murders, affaffina-tions, rapes* and *plunders* with which his three volumes abound. He then could not have difap-
pointed

pointed his friends by his total want of argument, as he now does in his two firſt eſſays; for on ſuch a ſubjeƈt no argument could be expeƈted; and in his third, where it is patiently attempted, he would have avoided the neceſſity of ſhowing that he has none, by giving a different title to his book; for the " appeal," inſtead of being " from the new to the old whigs," would have been *from the new whigs to the old tories*; and he might as well have appealed to Cæſar; he could have found at this day no court to take cognizance of his cauſe.

But the great advantage of this mode of handling the ſubjeƈt would have been, that it could have provoked no anſwers; the gauntlet might have been thrown, without a champion to have taken it up; and the laſt ſolitary admirer of chivalry have retired in negative triumph from the field.

Mr. Burke, however, in his defence of royalty, does not rely on this argument of the compaƈt. Whether it be, that he is conſcious of its futility, or that in his rage he forgets that he has uſed it, he he is perpetually recurring to the laſt ground that has yet been heard of, on which we are called upon to conſider kings even as a tolerable nuiſance, and to ſupport the exiſting forms of government: this ground is *the general good of the community*. It is ſaid to be dangerous to pull down ſyſtems that are already formed, or even to attempt to improve them; and it is likewiſe ſaid, that, were they peaceably deſtroyed, and we had ſociety to build up anew, it would be beſt to create hereditary kings, hereditary orders, and excluſive privileges.

Theſe are ſober opinions, uniting a claſs of rea-ſoners too numerous and too reſpectable to be treated with contempt. I believe however that their number is every day diminiſhing, and I be-lieve the example which France will ſoon be obliged to exhibit to the world on this ſubject, will induce every man to reject them, who is not perſonally and excluſively intereſted in their ſupport.

The inconſiſtency of the conſtituting aſſembly, in retaining an hereditary king, armed with an enor-mous civil liſt, to wage war with a popular go-vernment,

vernment, has induced fome perfons to predict the downfall of their conftitution. But this mea- fure had a different origin from what is commonly affigned to it, and will probably have a different iffue. It was the refult rather of local and tem- porary circumftances, than of any general belief in the utility of kings, under any modifications or limitations that could be attached to the office.

It is to be obferved, *firft*, that the French had a king upon their hands. This king had always been confidered as a well-difpofed man; fo that, by a fatality fomewhat fingular, though not un- exampled in *regal hiftory*, he gained the love of the people, almoft in proportion to the mifchief which he did them. *Secondly*, their king had very powerful family connexions, in the fovereigns of Spain, Auftria, Naples and Sardinia; befides his relations within the kingdom, whom it was necef- fary to attach, if poffible, to the interefts of the community. *Thirdly*, the revolution was confi- dered by all Europe as a high and dangerous ex- periment. It was neceffary to hide as much as poffible the appearance of its magnitude from the

C

eye

eye of the diftant obferver. The reformers confidered it as their duty to produce an internal re-
generation of fociety, rather than an external change
in the appearance of the court; to fet in order the
counting-houfe and the kitchen, before arranging
the drawing-room. This would leave the fovereigns of Europe totally without a pretext for in-
terfering; while it would be confoling to that clafs
of philofophers, who ftill believed in the compa-
tibility of royalty and liberty. *Fourthly*, this decree, That *France fhould have a king*, and that he
could do no wrong, was paffed at an early period of
their operations; when the above reafons were apparently more urgent than they were afterwards,
or probably will ever be again.

From thefe confiderations we may conclude,
that royalty is preferved in France for reafons which
are fugitive; that a majority of the conftituting
affembly did not believe in it, as an abftract principle; that a majority of the people will learn to
be difgufted with fo unnatural and ponderous a
deformity in their new edifice, and will foon hew
it off.   6

After

After this improvement fhall have been made, a few years experience in the face of Europe, and on fo great a theatre as that of France, will probably leave but one opinion in the minds of honeft men, relative to the republican principle, or the great fimplicity of nature applied to the organization of fociety.

The example of America would have had great weight in producing this conviction; but it is too little known to the European reafoner, to be a fubject of accurate inveftigation. Befides, the difference of circumftances between that country and the ftates of Europe has given occafion for imagining many diftinctions which exift not in fact, and has prevented the application of principles which are permanently founded in nature, and follow not the trifling variations in the ftate of fociety.

But I have not prefcribed to myfelf the tafk of entering into arguments on the utility of kings, or of inveftigating the meaning of Mr. Burke, in order to compliment him with an additional refutation. My fubject furnifhes a more extenfive

scope.

scope. It depends not on me, or Mr. Burke, or any other writer, or description of writers, to determine the question, whether a change of government shall take place, and extend through Europe. It depends on a much more important class of men, the class that cannot write; and in a great' measure, on those who cannot read. It is to be decided by men who reason better without books, than we do with all the books in the world. Taking it for granted, therefore, that a general revolution is at hand, whose progress is *irresistible*, my object is to contemplate its probable effects, and to comfort those who are afflicted at the prospect.

CHAP.

CHAP. I.

Feudal System.

THE moft prominent feature in the moral face of Europe, was imprinted upon it by conqueft. It is the refult of the fubordination neceffary among military favages, on their becoming cultivators of the foil which they had defolated, and making an advantageous ufe of fuch of the inhabitants as they did not choofe to maffacre, and could not fell to foreigners for flaves.

The relation thus eftablifhed between the officers and the foldiers, between the victors and the vanquifhed, and between them all and the lands which they were to cultivate, modified by the experience of unlettered ages, has obtained the name of the Feudal Syftem, and may be confidered as the foun-

dation

dation of all the political inftitutions in this quarter of the world. The claims refulting to particular claffes of men, under this modification of
fociety, are called Feudal Rights; and to the individual poffeffors they are either nominal or real,
conveying an empty title or a fubftantial profit.

My intention is not to enter on the details of
this fyftem, as a lawyer, or to trace its progrefs
with the accuracy of an hiftorian, and fhow its peculiar fitnefs to the rude ages of fociety which
gave it birth. But, viewing it as an ancient edifice, whofe foundation, worn away by the current
of events, can no longer fupport its weight, I
would fketch a few drawings, to fhow the ftyle of
its architecture, and compare it with the model of
the new building to be erected in its place.

The *philofophy* of the Feudal Syftem, is all that
remains of it worthy of our contemplation. This
I will attempt to trace in fome of its leading points,
leaving the practical part to fall, with its ancient
founders and its modern admirers, into the peaceful

ful gulph of oblivion; to which I wifh it a fpeedy and an unobftructed paffage.

The original object of this inftitution was un-doubtedly, what it was alledged to be, the prefer-vation of turbulent focieties, in which men are held together but by feeble ties; and it effected its purpofe by uniting the perfonal intereft of the head of each family, with the perpetual fafety of the ftate. Thus far the purpofe was laudable, and the means extremely well calculated for the end. But it was the fortune of this fyftem to attach itfelf to thofe paffions of human nature which vary not with the change of circumftances. While na-tional motives ceafed by degrees to require its continuance, family motives forbade to lay it afide. The fame progreffive improvements in fociety, which rendered military tenures and military titles firft unneceffary and then injurious to the general intereft, at the fame time fharpened the avarice, and piqued the honor of thofe who poffeffed them, to preferve the exclufive privileges which rendered them thus diftinguifhed. .And thefe privileges, united with the operations of the church, have

founded

founded and fupported the defpotifms of Europe in all their divifions, combinations and refinements.

Feudal Rights are either *territorial* or *perfonal*. I fhall divide them into thefe two claffes, for the fake of beftowing a few obfervations upon each.

The pernicious effects of the fyftem on territorial tenures are inconceivably various and great. In a legal view, it has led to thofe intricacies and vexations, which we find attached to every circumftance of real property, which have perplexed the fcience of civil jurifprudence, which have perpetuated the ignorance of the people relative to the adminiftration of juftice, rendered neceffary the intervention of lawyers, and multiplied the means of oppreffion. But, in a political view, its confequences are ftill more ferious, and demand a particular confideration.

The firft quality of the feudal tenure is to confine the defcendible property to the *eldeft male iffue*. To fay that this is contrary to nature, is but a

feeble

feeble expreſſion. So abominable is its operation, that it has ſeduced and perverted nature; her voice is ſtifled, intereſt itſelf is laid aſleep, and nothing but the eloquence of an incomprehenſible pride is heard on the occaſion. You will hear father and mother, younger brothers and ſiſters, rejoice in this proviſion of the law; the former conſigning their daughters to the gloomy priſon of a convent, and their younger ſons to the church or the army, to enſure their celibacy; that no remnant of the family may remain but the heir of the eſtate entire; the latter congratulating each other, that the elder brother will tranſmit unimpaired the title and the property, while they themſelves are content to periſh in the obſcurity of their ſeveral deſtinations. It is probable that, in another age, a tale of this kind will ſcarcely gain credit, and that the tear of ſenſibility may be ſpared by a diſbelief of the fact. It is however no creature of the imagination; it happened every day in France previous to the revolution; I have ſeen it with my own eyes and heard it with my own ears; it is now to be ſeen and heard in moſt other catholic countries,

But

But other points of view show this dispofition of the law to be still more reprehensible in the eye of political philofophy. It fwells the inequality of wealth, which, even in the best regulated fociety, is but too confiderable; it habituates the people to believe in an unnatural inequality in the rights of men, and by this means prepares them for fervility and oppreffion; it prevents the improvement of lands, and impedes the progrefs of induftry and cultivation, which are best promoted on fmall eftates, where proprietors cultivate for themfelves; it difcourages population, by inducing to a life of celibacy.—But I fhall fpeak of celibacy when I fpeak of the church.

Whether men are born to govern, or to obey, or to enjoy equal liberty, depends not on the original capacity of the mind, but on the *inftinct of analogy*, or the *habit of thinking*. When children of the fame family are taught to believe in the unconquerable diftinctions of birth among themfelves, they are completely fitted for a feudal government; becaufe their minds are familiarifed with all the gradations and degradations that fuch a go‐

vernment

vernment requires. The birth-right of domineer-
ing is not more readily claimed on the one hand,
than it is acknowledged on the other; and the
Jamaica planter is not more habitually convinced
that an European is fuperior to an African, than
he is that a lord is better than himfelf.

This fubject deferves to be placed in a light,
in which no writer, as far as I know, has yet confidered it. When a perfon was repeating to Fon-
tenelle the common adage *l'habitude eft la feconde
nature*, the philofopher replied, *Et faites moi la
grace de me dire, quelle eft la première*. When we
affert that nature has eftablifhed *inequalities* among
men, and has thus given to fome the right of governing others, or when we maintain the *contrary*
of this pofition, we fhould be careful to define
what fort of nature we mean, whether the *firft* or
fecond nature; or whether we mean that there is
but one. A mere favage, Colocolo * for inftance,
would decide the queftion of equality by a trial of
bodily ftrength, defignating the man that could

* See the Araucana of Ercilla.

lift

lift the heavieft beam to be the legiflator; and unlefs all men could lift the fame beam, they could not be equal in their rights. Ariftotle would give the preference to him that excelled in mental capacity. Ulyffes would make the decifion upon a compound ratio of both. But there appears to me another ftep in this ladder, and that the *habit of thinking* is the only fafe and univerfal criterion to which, in practice, the queftion can be referred. Indeed, when intereft is laid afide, it is the only one to which, in civilized ages, it ever is referred. We never fubmit to a king, becaufe he is ftronger than we in bodily force, nor becaufe he is fuperior in underftanding or in information; but becaufe we believe him born to govern, or at leaft, becaufe a majority of the fociety believes it.

This *habit of thinking* has fo much of nature in it, it is fo undiftinguifhable from the indelible marks of the man, that it is a perfectly fafe foundation for any fyftem that we may choofe to build upon it; indeed it is the *only* foundation, for it is the only point of contact by which men communicate as moral affociates. As a practical pofition

there-

therefore, and as relating to almoft all places and almoft all times, in which the experiment has yet been made, Ariftotle was as right in teaching, *That fome are born to command, and others to be commanded,* as the national affembly was in declaring, That *men are born and always continue free and equal in refpect to their rights.* The latter is as apparently falfe in the diet of Ratifbon, as the former is in the hall of the Jacobins.

Abftractedly confidered, there can be no doubt of the unchangeable truth of the affembly's declaration; and they have taken the right method to make it a *practical* truth, by publifhing it to the world for difcuffion. A general belief *that it is a truth,* makes it at once practical, confirms it in one nation, and extends it to others.

A due attention to the aftonifhing effects that are wrought in the world by *the habit of thinking,* will ferve many valuable purpofes. I cannot therefore difmifs the fubject fo foon as I intended; but will mention one or two inftances of thefe effects,

and

and leave the reflection of the reader to make the application to a thousand others.

First, It is evident that all the arbitrary systems in the world are founded and supported on this *second nature* of man, in counteraction of the *first*. Systems which distort and crush and subjugate every thing that we can suppose original and characteristic in man, as an undistorted being. It sustains the most absurd and abominable theories of religion, and honors them with as many martyrs as it does those that are the most peaceful and beneficent.

But *secondly*, we find for our consolation, that it will likewise support systems of equal liberty and national happiness. In the United States of America, the science of liberty is universally understood, felt and practised, as much by the simple as the wise, the weak as the strong. Their deep-rooted and inveterate habit of thinking is, that *all men are equal in their rights*, that *it is impossible to make them otherwise*; and this being their undisturbed belief, they have no conception how any

man

man in his senses can entertain any other. This point once settled, every thing is settled. Many operations, which in Europe have been considered as incredible tales or dangerous experiments, are but the infallible consequences of this great principle. The first of these operations is *the business of election*, which with that people is carried on with as much gravity as their daily labor. There is no jealousy on the occasion, nothing lucrative in office; any man in society may attain to any place in the government, and may exercise its functions. They believe that there is nothing more difficult in the management of the affairs of a nation, than the affairs of a family; that it only requires more hands. They believe that it is the juggle of keeping up impositions to blind the eyes of the vulgar, that constitutes the intricacy of state. Banish the mysticism of inequality, and you banish almost all the evils attendant on human nature.

The people, being habituated to the election of all kinds of officers, the *magnitude* of the office makes no difficulty in the case. The president of the United States, who has more power while in

office than fome of the kings of Europe, is chofen
with as little commotion as a churchwarden. There
is a public fervice to be performed, and the people fay who fhall do it. The fervant feels honored
with the confidence repofed in him, and generally
expreffes his gratitude by a faithful performance.

Another of thefe operations is making every
citizen a foldier, and every foldier a citizen; not
only *permitting* every man to arm, but *obliging* him
to arm. This fact, told in Europe previous to the
French revolution, would have gained little credit;
or at leaft it would have been regarded as a mark
of an uncivilized people, extremely dangerous to
a well ordered fociety. Men who build fyftems on
an inverfion of nature, are obliged to invert every
thing that is to make part of that fyftem. It is
*becaufe the people are civilized, that they are with
fafety armed.* It is an effect of their confcious
dignity, as citizens enjoying equal rights, that they
wifh not to invade the rights of others. The danger (where there is any) from armed citizens, is
only to the *government*, not to the *fociety*; and as
long as they have nothing to revenge in the government

vernment (which they cannot have while it is in their own hands) there are many advantages in their being accuſtomed to the uſe of arms, and no poſſible diſadvantage.

Power, habitually in the hands of a whole com‑munity, loſes all the ordinary aſſociated ideas of power. The exerciſe of power is a relative term; it ſuppoſes an oppoſition,—ſomething to operate upon. We perceive no exertion of power in the motion of the planetary ſyſtem, but a very ſtrong one in the movement of a whirlwind; it is becauſe we ſee obſtructions to the latter, but none to the former. Where the government is *not* in the hands of the people, there you find oppoſition, you per‑ceive two contending intereſts, and get an idea of the exerciſe of power; and whether this power be in the hands of the government or of the people, or whether it change from ſide to ſide, it is always to be dreaded. But the word *people* in America has a different meaning from what it has in Eu‑rope. It there means the whole community, and comprehends every human creature; here it means ſomething elſe, more difficult to define.

Another

Another confequence of the habitual idea of equality, is the *facility of changing the ftructure of their government* whenever and as often as the fociety fhall think there is any thing in it to amend. As Mr. Burke has written no " reflections on the revolution" in America, the people there have never yet been told that they had no *right* " to frame a government for themfelves;" they have therefore done much of this bufinefs, without ever affixing to it the idea of " facrilege" or " ufurpation," or any other term of rant to be found in that gentleman's vocabulary.

Within a few years the fifteen ftates have not only framed each its own ftate-conftitution, and two fucceffive federal conftitutions; but fince the fettlement of the prefent general government in the year 1789, three of the ftates, Pennfylvania, South-Carolina and Georgia, have totally new modeled their own. And all this is done without the leaft confufion ; the operation being fcarcely known beyond the limits of the ftate where it is performed. Thus they are in the habit of " *choofing their own governors,*" of " *cafhiering them for mifconduct,*"

of

of "*framing a government for themselves*," and all those abominable things, the mere naming of which, in Mr. Burke's opinion, has polluted the pulpit in the Old Jewry.

But it is said, These things will do very well for America, where the people are less numerous, less indigent, and better instructed; but they will not apply to Europe. This objection deserves a reply, not because it is solid, but because it is fashionable. It may be answered, that some parts of Spain, much of Poland, and almost the whole of Russia, are less peopled than the settled country in the United States; that poverty and ignorance are *effects* of slavery rather than its *causes*; but the best answer to be given, is the example of France. To the event of that revolution I will trust the argument. Let the people have time to become thoroughly and soberly grounded in the doctrine of *equality*, and there is no danger of oppression either from government or from anarchy. Very little instruction is necessary to teach a man his rights; and there is no person of common intellects in the most ignorant corner of Europe, but

receives

receives leſſons enough, if they were of the proper kind. For writing and reading are not indifpen-ſible to the object ; it is *thinking* right which makes them act right. Every child is taught to repeat about fifty Latin prayers, which ſet up the Pope, the Biſhop, and the King, as the trinity of his ado-ration ; he is taught that *the powers that be are ordained of God,* and therefore the ſoldier quartered in the pariſh has a right to cut his throat. Half this inftruction, upon oppofite principles, would go a great way ; in that caſe Nature would be aſſiſted, while here ſhe is counteracted. Engrave it on the heart of a man, *that all men are equal in rights,* and that the *government is their own,* and then perſuade him to ſell his crucifix and buy a muſquet,—and you have made him a good citizen.

Another conſequence of a ſettled belief in the equality of rights, is, that under this belief *there is no danger from Anarchy.* This word has likewiſe acquired a different meaning in America from what we read of it in books. In Europe it means confuſion, attended with mobs and carnage, where the innocent periſh with the guilty. But it is very

different

different where a country is *used* to a reprefentative
government, though it fhould have an interval of
no government at all. Where the people at large
feel and know that they *can do every thing* by
themfelves perfonally, they. really *do nothing* by
themfelves perfonally. In the heat of the American revolution, when the people in fome ftates
were for a long time without the leaft fhadow of
law or government, they always acted by com-
mittees and reprefentation. This they muft call
anarchy, for they know no other.

Thefe are materials for the formation of governments, which need not be dreaded, though dif-
jointed and laid afunder to make fome repairs.
They are deep-rooted habits of thinking, which
almoft change the moral nature of man ; they are
principles as much unknown to the ancient republics as to the modern monarchies of Europe.

We muft not therefore rely upon fyftems drawn
from the experimental reafonings of Ariftotle, when
we find them contradicted by what we feel to be
the eternal truth of nature, and fee brought to

the

the teft of our own experience. Ariftotle was certainly a great politician; and Claudius Ptolemy
was a great geographer; but the latter has faid
not a word of America, the largeft quarter of the
globe; nor the former, of reprefentative republics,
the refource of afflicted humanity.

Since I have brought thefe two great lumina-
ries of fcience fo near together, I will keep them
in company a moment longer, to fhow the ftrange
partiality that we may retain for one fuperftition
after having laid afide another, though they are
built on fimilar foundations. Ptolemy wrote a
fyftem of aftronomy; in which he taught, among
other things, that the earth was the centre of the
univerfe, and that the heavenly bodies moved
round it. This fyftem is now taught (to the exclufion by anathema of all others) in Turkey, Ara-
bia, Perfia, Paleftine, Egypt, and wherever the
doctrines of Mahomet are taught; while at the
fame time, and with the fame reverence, the politics
of Ariftotle are taught at the univerfity of Oxford.
The ground which fupports the one is, that the
fun ftopt its courfe at the command of Jofhua, .

6   which

which it could not have done, had it not been in motion; and the other, that *the powers that be are ordained of God.* Mention to a Muſſulman the Copernican ſyſtem, and you might aſ well ſpeak to Mr. Burke about the rights of man; they both call you an atheiſt.—But I will proceed with the feudal ſyſtem.

The next quality of a feudal tenure is what is commonly called on the continent the right of *ſubſtitution,* in the Engliſh law, known by the name of *entail.* Of all the methods that have yet been diſcovered to prevent men from enjoying the advantages that nature has laid before them, this is the moſt extraordinary, and in many reſpects the moſt effectual. There have been ſuperſtitions entertained by many nations relative to property in lands; rendering them more difficult of alienation than other poſſeſſions, and conſequently, leſs productive. Such was the *jus retraćtus* of the Romans, the family-right of redemption, and the abſolute reſtoration once in fifty years among the Jews, ſimilar regulations among the ancient Egyp-

tians,

tians, and laws to the fame purpofe under the government of the Incas in Peru.

Thefe were all calculated to perpetuate family
diftinctions, and to temper the minds of men to
an ariftocratical fubordination. But none of them
were attended with the barbarous exclufion of
younger brothers; nor had they the prefumption
to put it into the power of a dying man, who
could not regulate the difpofition of his fandals
for one hour, to fay to all mankind thenceforward
to the end of time, " Touch not my inheritance !
I will that this tract of country, on which I have
taken my pleafure, fhall remain to the wild beafts
and to the fowls of heaven; that one man only of
each generation fhall exift upon it; that all the reft,
even of my own pofterity, fhall be driven out
hence as foon as born; and that the inheritor himfelf fhall not increafe his enjoyments by alienating
a part to ameliorate the reft."

There might have been individual madmen in
all ages, capable of *expreffing* a defire of this kind;
but

but for whole nations, for many centuries together, to agree to *reverence* and *execute* such hostile testaments as these, comported not with the wisdom of the ancients; it is a suicide of society, reserved for the days of chivalry,—to support the governments of modern Europe.

Sir Edward Coke should have spared his panegyric on the parliament of Edward the first as the fathers of the law of entailments. He quotes with singular pleasure the words of Sir William Herle, who informs us that " King Edward I. was the " wisest king that ever was, and they were sage " men who made this statute." Whatever wisdom there is in the statute, is of an elder growth. It is a plant of genuine feudal extraction brought into England by the Normans or Saxons, or some other conquerors; and though settled as common law, it began to be disregarded and despised by the judicial tribunals, as a sense of good policy prevailed. But the progress of liberality was arrested by that parliament, and the law of entailments passed into the statute of Westminster the second.

This was confidered as law in America, previous to the revolution. But that epoch of light
and liberty has freed one quarter of the world from
this miferable appendage of Gothicifm; and France
has now begun to break the fhackles from another
quarter, where they were more ftrongly rivetèd.
The fimple deftruction of thefe two laws, of *entail-
ment* and *primogeniture*, if you add to it the *freedom
of the prefs*, will enfure the continuance of liberty
in any country where it is once eftablifhed!

Other territorial rights, peculiar to the feudal
tenure, are lefs general in their operation, though
almoft infinite in their number and variety. Not
a current of water, nor a mill-feat, nor a fifh-pond,
nor a foreft, nor the dividing line of a village or a
farm; but gives name to and fupports fome feig-
neurial impofition; befides the numberlefs claims'
predicated upon all the poffible actions and cere-
monies that pafs, or are fuppofed to pafs, between
the great lord and the little lord, and between the
little lord and the lefs lord, and between him and
the Lord knows whom. The national affembly in
one decree fuppreffed about one hundred and fifty

of thefe taxes by name, befides a general fweep-
ing claufe in the act, which perhaps deftroyed
as many more, the names of which no man could
report.

One general character will apply to all thefe
impofitions: they are a difcouragement to agriculture, an embarraffment to commerce,—they
humiliate one part of the community, fwell the
pride of the other, and are a real pecuniary difad-
vantage to both.

But it is time to pay our refpects to thofe feudal
claims that we call *perfonal*. The firft of thefe is
allegiance,—in its genuine Gothic fenfe, called *perpetual allegiance*. It is difficult to exprefs a fuitable
contempt for this idea, without defcending to lan-
guage below the dignity of philofophy. On the
firft invefiture of a fief, the fuperior lord (fup-
pofing he had any right to it himfelf) has doubtlefs the power of granting it on whatever terms
the vaffal will agree to. It is an even bargain
between the parties; and an unchangeable allegiance
during the lives of thefe parties may be a condi-

tio?

tion of it. But for a man to be *born* to fuch an allegiance to another man, is to have an evil ftar indeed; it is to be born to unchangeable flavery.

A nobleman of Tufcany, at this moment, cannot ftep his foot over the limits of the duchy without leave from the Grand Duke, on pain of forfeiting his eftate. Similar laws prevail in all feudal countries, where revolutions have not yet prevailed. They flee before the fearching eye of liberty,, and will foon flee from Europe.

Hitherto we have treated of claims, whether perfonal or territorial, that are confined to the eldeft fons of families; but there is one genuine feudal claim, which " fpreads undivided" to all the children, runs in all collateral directions, and extends to every drop of noble blood, wherever found, however mixt or adulterated,—it is the claim of *idlenefs*. In general it is fuppofed that all indigent noble children are to be provided for by the government. But alas ! the fwarm is too great to be eafily hived. Though the army, the navy,

and

and the church, with all their poffible multiplication of places, are occupied only by them, yet, as celibacy deprives them not of the means of propagation, the number continues fo confiderable, that many remain out of employment and deftitute of the means of fupport.

In contemplating the peculiar deftiny of this defcription of men, we cannot but feel a mixture of emotions, in which compaffion gets the better of contempt. In addition to the misfortunes incident to other claffes of fociety, their noble birth has entailed upon them a fingular curfe; it has interdicted them every kind of bufinefs or occupation, even for procuring the neceffaries of life. Other men may be found who have been deprived of their juft inheritance by the barbarous laws of defcent, who may have been neglected in youth and not educated to bufinefs, or who by averfion to induftry are rendered incapable of any ufeful employment; but none but the offspring of a noble family can experience the fuperadded fatality of being told, that to put his hand to the plough, or

his

his foot into a counting-houſe, would diſgrace an illuſtrious line of anceſtors, and wither a tree of genealogy, which takes its root in a groom of ſome fortunate robber, who perhaps was an archer of Charlemagne.

Every capital in Europe, if you except London, throngs with this miſerable claſs of nobleſſe, who are really and literally tormented between their pride and their poverty. Indeed, ſuch is the pre-poſterous tyranny of cuſtom, that thoſe who are rich, and take the lead in ſociety, have the cruelty to make *idleneſs* a *criterion of nobleſſe.* A proof of inoccupation is a ticket of admiſſion into their houſes, and an indiſpenſible badge of welcome to their parties.

But in France their hands are at laſt untied; the charm is broken, and the feudal ſyſtem, with all its infamous idolatries, has fallen to the ground. Honor is reſtored to the heart of man, inſtead of being ſuſpended from his button-hole; and uſeful induſtry gives a title to reſpect. The men that

were

were formerly dukes and marquiffes are now exalted to farmers, manufacturers and merchants; the rifing generation among all claffes of people are forming their maxims on a juft eftimate of things; and Society is extracting the poifoned dagger which conqueft had planted in her vitals.

CHAP.

CHAP. II.

The Church.

BUT it would have been impoffible for the feudal fyftem, with all its powers of inver-fion, to have held human nature fo long debafed, without the aid of an agent more powerful than an arm of flefh, and without affailing the mind with other weapons than thofe which are furnifhed from its temporal concerns. Mankind are by nature religious; the governors of nations, or thofe per-fons who contrive to live upon the labors of their fellow-creatures, muft neceffarily be few, in com-parifon to thofe who bear the burthens of the whole; their objeƈt therefore is to dupe the community at large, to conceal the ftrength of the many, and magnify that of the few. An open arrangement of forces, whether phyfical or moral, muft be artfully

avoided;

avoided; for men, however ignorant, are as naturally difpofed to calculation, as they are to religion; they perceive as readily that an hundred foldiers can deftroy the captain they have made, as that thunder and lightning can deftroy a man. Recourfe muft therefore be had to myfteries and invifibilities; an engine muft be forged out of the *religion* of human nature, and erected on its *credulity*, to play upon and extinguifh the light of reafon, which was placed in the mind as a caution to the one and a kind companion to the other.

This engine, in all ages of the world, has been the Church *. It' has varied its appellation, at
. different

* From that affociation of ideas, which ufually connects the *church* with *religion*, I may run the rifque of being mifunderftood by fome readers, unlefs I advertife them, that I confider no connection as exifting between thefe two fubjects; and that where I fpeak of church *indefinitely*, I mean the government of a ftate, affuming the name of God, to govern by divine authority; or, in other words, *darkening the confciences of men, in order to opprefs them.*

In the United States of America, there is, ftrictly fpeaking, no fuch thing as a Church; and yet in no country are the peopl:

more

different periods and in different countries, according to the circumſtances of nations; but has never changed its character; and it is difficult to ſay, under which of its names it has done the moſt miſchief, and exterminated the greateſt number of the human race. Were it not for the danger of being miſled by the want of information, we ſhould readily determine, that under the aſſumption of chriſtianity it has committed greater ravages than under any other of its dreadful denominations.

But we muſt not be haſty in deciding this queſtion; as, during the laſt fifteen centuries, in which we are able to trace with compaſſionate indignation the frenzy of our anceſtors, and contemplate the wandering demon of carnage, con-

more religious. All ſorts of religious opinions are entertained there, and yet no *hereſy* among them all; all modes of worſhip are practiſed, and yet there is no *ſchiſm*; men frequently change their creed and their worſhip, and yet there is no *apoſtaſy*; they have miniſters of religion, but no *prieſts*. In ſhort, religion is there a *perſonal* and not a *corporate* concern.

ducted by the *cro/s* of the West, the lights of history fail us with regard to the rest of the world,— we cannot travel with the *crescent* of the East, in its unmeafurable devastations from the Euxine to the Ganges; nor tell by what other incantations mankind have been inflamed with the luft of flaughter, from thence to the north of Siberia or to the fouth of Africa.

Could we form an eftimate of the lives loft in the wars and perfecutions of the Chriftian Church alone, it muft be nearly equal to the number of fouls now exifting in Europe. But it is perhaps in mercy to mankind, that we are not able to calculate, with any accuracy, even this portion of human calamities. When Conftantine ordered that the *hierarchy* fhould affume the name of Chrift, we are not to confider him as forming a new weapon of deftruction; he only changed a name, which had grown into difrepute, and would ferve the purpofe no longer, for one that was gaining an extenfive reputation; it being built on a faith that was likely to meet the affent of a confiderable portion

of

of mankind. The cold-hearted * cruelty of that monarch's character, and his embracing the new doctrines with a temper hardened in the slaughter of

---

* The report of Zofimus refpecting the motives which induced Conftantine to embrace Chriftianity, has not been generally credited, though the circumftance is probable in itfelf, and the author is confidered in other refpects an hiftorian of undoubted veracity ; having written the hiftory of all the emperors, down to his own time, which was the beginning of the fifth century. His account is, That Conftantine could not be admitted into the *old eftablifhed church of Ceres* at Eleufis, on account of the enormity of his crimes, in the murder of many of his own family. But on his demanding admiffion, the Hyerophant cried out with horror, " Be gone, thou parricide, whom the gods will not pardon." The Chriftian doctors feized this occafion to adminifter to the wants of the emperor, on condition that he would adminifter to theirs ; the bargain was advantageous on both fides ; he declared himfelf a Chriftian, and took the church under his protection, and they pronounced his pardon.

The fawning fervility of the new church and the blunt feverity of the old, on that occafion, mark the precife character of the ecclefiaftical policy of all ages ; and both examples have been followed in numerous inftances. The manœuvres of the Pope on the converfion of Clovis, on fanctioning the ufurpa-

of his relations, were omens unfavorable to the future complexion of the hierarchy; though he had, thus coupled it with a name that had hitherto been remarkable for its mildnefs and humiliation. This tranfaction has therefore given colour to a fcene of enormities, which may be regarded as nothing more than the genuine offspring of the *alliance of Church and State.*

This fatal deviation from the principles of the firft founder of the faith, who declared that his *kingdom was not of this world,* has deluged Europe in blood for a long fucceffion of ages, and carried occafional ravages into all the other quarters of the globe. The pretence of extirpating the idolatries of ancient eftablifhments and the innumerable herefies of the new, has been the never-failing argu-

tion of Pepin, and on the coronation of Charlemagne, are among the imitations of the former; the ridiculous chaftifement of Henry the Second of England, and the numerous anathemas fulminated againft whole kingdoms, are proofs of the latter. We may likewife remark, that the conduct of Conftantine has been copied in all its effential points by Henry the Eighth.

ment

ment of princes as well as pontiffs, from the wars
of Conftantine, down to the pitiful, ftill-born rebellion of Calonne and the Count d'Artois.

From the time of the converfion of Clovis,
through all the Merovingian race, France and
Germany groaned under the fury of ecclefiaftical
monfters, hunting down the Druids, overturning
the temples of the Roman Polytheifts, and drench-
ing the plains with the blood of Arians *. The
wars of Charlemagne againft the Saxons, the Huns,
the Lombards and the Moors, which defolated
Europe for forty years, had for their principal object the extending and purifying of the Chriftian
faith. The Crufades, which drained Europe of its

* Exterminating heretics was a principal object of national
ambition. Childebert I. who died in 558, has the following
epitaph on his tomb in the Abbey of *St. Germaine des Prés*, at
Paris.

> *Le fang des Arriens dont rougirent les plaines,*
> *De montagnes de corps leur pays tout couvert,*
> *Et leurs chefs mis à mort, font des preuves certaines*
> *De ce que les François firent fous Childebert.*

young

young men at eight fucceffive periods, muft have
facrificed, including Afiatics and Africans, at leaft
four millions of lives. The wars of the Guelfs and
Gibelins, or Pope and Anti-Pope, ravaged Italy,
and involved half Europe in factions for two centuries together. The expulfion of the Moors from
Spain depopulated that kingdom by a war of
feven hundred years, and eftablifhed the Inquifi-
tion to interdict the refurrection of fociety; while
millions of the natives of South America have
been deftroyed by attempting to convert them.

In this enumeration, we have taken no notice
of that train of calamities which attended the re-
converfion of the eaftern empire, and attaching it
to the faith of Mahomet; nor of the various havoc
which followed the difmemberment of the catholic
church by that fortunate fchifm, which by fome
is denominated the Lutheran herefy, and by others
the Proteftant reformation.

But thefe, it will be faid, are only general traits
of uncivilized character, which we all contemplate
with equal horror, and which, among enlightened

nations,

nations, there can be no danger of feeing renewed.
It is true, that in feveral countries, the glooms of
intolerance feem to be pierced by the rays of philofophy; and we may foon expect to fee Europe
univerfally difclaiming the right of one man to in-
terfere in the religion of another. We may remark however, *firft*, that this is far from being the
cafe at this moment; and *fecondly*, that it is a
bleffing which never can originate from any ftate-
eftablifhment of religion. For proofs of the former, we need not penetrate into Spain or Italy, nor
recal the hiftory of the late fanatical management
of the war in Brabant,—but look to the two moft
enlightened countries in Europe; fee the riots at
Birmingham, and the conduct of the refractory
priefts in France.

With regard to the fecond remark,—we may as
well own the truth at firft as at laft, and have
fenfe this year as the next: *The exiftence of any kind*
of liberty is incompatible with the exiftence of any kind
of church. By *liberty* I mean the enjoyment of
equal rights, and by *church* I mean any mode of
worfhip

worſhip declared to be national, or declared to have any preference in the eye of the law.

To render this truth a little more familiar to the mind of any reader who ſhall find himſelf ſtartled with it, we will take a view of the church in a different light from what we have yet con-ſidered it. We have noticed hitherto only its moſt ſtriking characteriſtics, in which it appears like a giant, ſtalking over ſociety, and wielding the fword of ſlaughter; but it likewiſe performs the office of ſilent diſeaſe and of unperceived de-cay; where we may contemplate it as a canker, corroding the vitals of the moral world, and de-baſing all that is noble in man.

If I mention ſome traits which are rather pecu-liar to the Roman Catholic conſtitution, it is be-cauſe that is the predominant church in thoſe parts of Europe, where revolutions are ſooneſt expect-ed; and not becauſe it is any worſe or any better than any other that ever has or ever can exiſt. I hinted before, and it may not be amiſs to repeat, that the hierarchy is every where the ſame, ſo far

as the circumstances of society will permit; for it
borrows and lends, and interchanges its features in
some measure with the age and nat'on with which
it has to deal, without ever losing sight of its object. It is every where the same engine of state;
and whether it be guided by a Lama or a Mufti,
by a Pontifex or a Pope, by a Bramin, a Bishop
or a Druid, it is entitled to an equal share of
respect.

The first great object of the priest is to establish
a belief in the minds of the people, that *he himself
is possest of supernatural powers*; and the church at
all times has made its way in the world, in proportion as the priest has succeeded in this particular. This is the foundation of every thing,—
the life and soul of all that is subversive and unaccountable in human affairs; it is introducing a
new element into society; it is the rudder under
the water, steering the ship almost directly contrary to the wind that gives it motion.

A belief in the supernatural powers of the priest
has been inspired by means, which in different
nations

nations'have-been known by different names,— such as aftrologies, auguries, oracles or incantations. This article once eftablifhed, its continuation is not a difficult tafk. For as the church acquires wealth, it furnifhes itfelf with the neceffary apparatus, and the trade is carried on to advantage. The impofition too becomes more eafy from the authority of precedent, by which the inquifitive faculties of the mind are benumbed; men believe by prefcription, and orthodoxy is hereditary.

In this manner every nation of antiquity received the poifon in its infancy, and was rendered incapable of acquiring a vigorous manhood, of fpeaking a national will, or of acting with that dignity and generofity, which are natural to man in fociety. The moment that Romulus confulted the oracles for the building of his city, that moment he interdicted its future citizens the enjoyment of liberty among themfelves, as well as all ideas of juftice towards their neighbours. Men never act their own opinions, in company with thofe who can give them the opinions of gods; and as long as governors have an eftablifhed mode of confulting the aufpices, there is no neceffity to eftablifh any mode of confulting the people. *Nihil publice fine aufpiciis nec domi nec militiæ gerebatur* *, was the Roman *Magna Charta*; and it ftood in place of a declaration of the rights of man. There is fomething extremely impofing in a maxim of this kind. Nothing is more pious, peaceful, and moderate in appearance; and nothing more favage and abominable in its operation. But it is a genuine *churchmaxim*, and, as fuch, deferves a further confideration,

One obvious tendency of this maxim is, like the feudal rights, to inculcate radical ideas of inequalities among men; and it does this in a much greater degree. The feudal diftance between man and man is perceptible and definite; but the moment you give one member of fociety a familiar intercourfe with God, you launch him into the region of infinities and invifibilities; you unfit him and his brethren to live together on any terms but thofe of ftupid reverence and of infolent abufe.

* *Cicero de divinatione.* Lib. I.

Another

Another tendency is to make men cruel and
favage in a preternatural degree. When a perfon
believes that he is doing the immediate work of
God, he divefts himfelf of the feelings of a man.
And an ambitious general, who wifhes to extirpate
or to plunder a neighbouring nation, has only to
order the prieft to do his duty and fet the people at
work by an oracle; they then know no other bounds
to their frenzy than the will of their leader, pronounced by the prieft; whofe voice to them is the
voice of God. In this cafe the leaft attention to
mercy or juftice would be abhorred as a difobedi-
ence to the divine command. This circumftance
alone is fufficient to account for two-thirds of the
cruelty of all wars,—perhaps in a great meafure
for their exiftence,—and has given rife to an opinion, that nations are cruel in proportion as they
are religious. But the obfervation ought to ftand
thus, *That nations are cruel in proportion as they are
guided by priefts;* than which there is no axiom
more undeniably without exception.

Another tendency of governing men by oracles,
is to make them factious and turbulent in the ufe

of

of liberty, when they feel themselves in poffeffion of it. In all ancient democracies, the great body of the people enjoyed no liberty at all; and thofe who were called freemen exercifed it only by ftarts, for the purpofe of *revenging* injuries,—not in a regular conftituted mode of *preventing* them; the body politic ufed liberty as a medicine, and not as daily bread. Hence it has happened, that the hiftory of ancient democracies and of modern infurrections are quoted upon us, to the infult of common fenfe, to prove that a whole people is not capable of governing itfelf. The whole of the reafoning on this fubject, from the profound difquifitions of Ariftotle, down to the puny whinings of Dr. Tatham *, are founded on a direct inverfion of hiftorical fact. It is the *want* of liberty, and not the *enjoyment* of it, which has occafioned all the factions in fociety from the beginning of

---

* It may be neceffary to inform the reader, that Dr. Tatham of Oxford has written a book in defence of Royalty and Mr. Burke. As this is the laft as well as weakeft thing againft liberty that I have met with, it is mentioned in the text for the fake of widening the grafp of my affertion, as well as for heightening the contraft among all poffible authors.

time, and will do so to the end; it is because the people are *not* habitually free from civil and ecclesiastical tyrants, that they are disposed to exercise tyranny themselves. Habitual freedom produces effects directly the reverse in every particular. For a proof of this, look into America; or if that be too much trouble, look into human nature with the eyes of common sense.

When the Christian religion was perverted and pressed into the service of Government, under the name of the *Christian Church*, it became necessary that its priests should set up for supernatural powers, and invest themselves in the same cloak of infallibility, of which they had stripped their predecessors, the Druids and the Augurs. This they effected by miracles; for which they gained so great a reputation, that they were canonized after death, and have furnished modern Europe with a much greater catalogue of saints, than could be found in any breviary of the ancients. The polytheism of the Catholic Church is more splendid for the number of its divinities, than that of the Eleusinian; and they are not inferior in point of attributes.

butes. The Denis of France is at leaſt equal to the Jupiter of Greece or the Apis of Egypt. As to ſupernatural powers, the caſe is preciſely the ſame in both; and the portions of infallibility are dealt out from the pope to the ſubordinate prieſts, according to their rank, in ſuch a manner as to complete the harmony of the ſyſtem.

Cicero has written with as much judgment and erudition on the " corruptions" of the old Roman Church, as Dr. Prieſtley has on thoſe of the new. But it is not the *church* which is corrupted by men, it is *men* who are corrupted by the church; for the very exiſtence of a church, as I have before defined it, is founded on a lie; it ſets out with the blaſphemy of giving to one claſs of men the attributes of God; and the practiſing of theſe forceries by that claſs, and believing them by another, corrupts and vitiates the whole.

One of the moſt admirable contrivances of the Chriſtian church is the buſineſs of *confeſſions*. It requires great reflection to give us an idea of the effects wrought on ſociety by this part of the machinery.

machinery. It is a solemn recognition of the supernatural powers of the priest, repeated every day
in the year by every human creature above the
age of twelve years. Nothing is more natural
than for men to judge of every thing around them,
and even of themselves, by *comparison*; and in
this case what opinion are the laity to form of their
own dignity? When a poor, ignorant, vicious mor-
tal is set up for the *God*, what is to be the *man?*
I cannot conceive of any person going seriously to
a confessional, and believing in the equality of
rights, or possessing one moral sentiment that is
worthy of a rational being *.

* The following tariff of the prices of absolution will show
what ideas these holy fathers have inculcated relative to the
proportional degree of moral turpitude in different crimes. It
was reprinted at Rome no longer ago than the last century.

For a layman who shall strike a priest without effu- sion of blood	£0	5	0
For one layman who shall kill another	0		
For murdering a father, mother, wife or sister			
For eating meat in Lent		5	5
For him who lies with his mother or sister	0	3	8
For marrying on those days when the Church for- bids matrimony	2	0	0
For the absolution of all crimes	2	16	0

Another

Another contrivance of the fame fort, and little inferior in efficacy, is the law of *celibacy* impofed on the priefthood, both male and female, in almoft all church-eftablifhments that have hitherto ex-ifted. The prieft is in the firft place armed with the weapons of moral deftruction, by which he is made the profeffional enemy of his fellow men; and then, for fear he fhould neglect to ufe thofe weapons,—for fear he fhould contract the feelings and friendfhips of rational beings, by mingling with fociety and becoming one of its members, —for fear his impofitions fhould be difcovered by the intimacy of family connections,—he is inter-dicted the moft cordial endearments of life; he is fevered from the fympathies of his fellow-creatures, and yet compelled to be with them; his affections are held in the *mortmain* of perpetual inactivity; and, like the dead men of Mezentius, he is lafhed to fociety for tyranny and contamination.

The whole of this management, in felecting, preparing and organizing the members of the ec-clefiaftical body, is purfued with the fame uniform, cold-blooded hoftility againft the focial harmonies

of

of life. The fubjects are taken from the younger
fons of noble families, who from their birth are
confidered as a nuifance to the houfe, and an out-
caft from parental attachment. They are then
cut off from all opportunities of forming fraternal
affections, and educated in a cloifter; till they
enter upon their public functions, as difconnected
from the feelings of the community, as it is de-
figned they fhall ever remain from its interefts.

I will not mention the corruption of morals,
which muft refult from the combined caufes of the
ardent paffions of conftrained celibacy, and the
fecret interviews of the prieft with the women of
his charge, for the purpofe of confeffions; I will
draw no arguments from the diffenfions fown in
families; the jealoufies and confequent aberrations
of both hufband and wife, occafioned by an in-
triguing ftranger being in the fecrets of both; the
difcouragements laid upon matrimony by a general
dread of thefe confequences in the minds of men
of reflection,—effects which are remarkable in all
catholic countries; but I will conclude this article
by obferving the direct influence that ecclefiaftical

celibacy

celibacy alone has had on the population of Europe.

This policy of the church muſt have produced at leaſt as great an effect, in thinning ſociety, as the whole of her wars and perſecutions. In Catholic Europe there muſt be near a million of ecclefiaſtics. This proportion of mankind continuing deducted from the agents of population for fifteen centuries, muſt have precluded the exiſtence of more than one hundred millions of the human ſpecies.

Should the reader be difpofed on this remark to liſten to the reply which is ſometimes made, that Europe is ſufficiently populous; I beg he would fufpend his decifion, till he ſhall fee what may be faid, in the courfe of this work, on protected induſtry; and until he ſhall well confider the effects of liberty on the means of fubfiſtence. That reply is certainly one of the axioms of tyranny, and is of kin to the famous wiſh of Caligula, that the whole Roman people had but one neck.

The

The French have gone as far in the deftruction of the hierarchy as could have been expected, confidering the habits of the people and the prefent circumftances of Europe. The church in that country was like royalty,—the prejudices in its favor were too ftrong to be vanquifhed all at once. The moft that could be done, was to tear the bandage from the eyes of mankind, break the charm of inequality, demolifh ranks and infallibilities, and teach the people that mitres and crowns did not confer fupernatural powers. As long as public teachers are chofen by the people, are falaried and removeable by the people, are born and married among the people, have families to be educated and protected from oppreffion and from vice,—as long as they have all the common fympathies of fociety to bind them to the public intereft, there is very little danger of their becoming tyrants by force; and the liberty of the prefs will prevent their being fo by craft.

In the United States of America there is no church; and this is one of the principal circumftances which diftinguifh that government from

all

all others that ever exifted; it enfures the un-em-
barraffed exercife of religion, the continuation of
public inftruction in the fcience of liberty and happinefs, and promifes a long duration to a reprefentative government,

CHAP.

CHAP. III.

————————

THE MILITARY SYSTEM.

Il importoit au maintien de l'autorité du roi, d'entre-
tenir la guerre,   Histoire de Charlemagne.

THE church, in all modern Europe, may be
considered as a kind of standing army; as
the members of that community have been in
every nation, the surest supporters of arbitrary
power, both for internal oppression and for external violence. But this not being sufficient of itself,
an additional instrument, to be known by the name
of the *military system*, became necessary; and it
seems to have been expedient to call up another
element of human nature, out of which this new
instrument might be created and maintained. The

church

church was in poffeffion of the ftrongeft ground that could be taken in the human mind, the *principle of religion*; a principle dealing with things invifible; and confequently the moft capable of being itfelf perverted, and then of perverting the whole mind, and fubjecting it to any unreafonable purfuit.

Next to that of religion, and fimilar to it in moft of its characteriftics, is the principle of *honor*. Honor, like religion, is an original, indelible fentiment of the mind, an indifpenfable ingredient in our nature. But its object is incapable of precife definition; and confequently, though given us in aid of the more definable feelings of morality, it is capable of total perverfion, of lofing fight of its own original nature, and ftill retaining its name; of purfuing the deftruction of moral fentiments, inftead of being their ornament; of debafing, inftead of fupporting, the dignity of man.

This camelion principle was therefore a proper element of impofition, and was deftined to

make

make an immenfe figure in the world, as the foundation and fupport of the military fyftem of all
unequal governments. We muft look pretty far
into human nature, before we fhall difcover the
caufe, why killing men in battle fhould be deem-
ed, *in itfelf*, an honorable employment. A hang-
man is univerfally defpifed; he exercifes an office
which not only the feelings but the policy of all
nations have agreed to regard as infamous. What
is it that fhould make the difference of thefe two
occupations in favor of the former? Surely it is
not becaufe the victims in the former cafe are *innocent*, and in the latter *guilty*. To affert this,
would be a greater libel upon human fociety than
I can bring myfelf to utter; it would make the
tyranny of opinion the moft *deteftable*, as well as
the moft fovereign of all poffible tyrannics. But
what can it be? It is not, what is fometimes alledged, that *courage* is the foundation of the bufinefs; that fighting is honorable becaufe it is dangerous; there is often as much courage difplayed
in highway-robbery, as in the warmeft conflict of
armies; and yet it does no honor to the party; a
Robin Hood is as difhonorable a character as a

Jack

Jack Ketch. It is not becaufe there is any idea of *juftice* or *honefty* in the cafe; for to fay the beft that can be faid of war, it is impoffible that more than one fide can be juft or honeft; and yet both fides of every conteft are equally the road to fame; where a diftinguifhed killer of men is fure to gain immortal honor. It is not *patriotifm*, even in that fenfe of the word which deviates the moft from general philanthropy; for a total ftranger to both parties in a war, may enter into it on either fide as a volunteer, perform more than a vulgar fhare of the flaughter, and be for ever applauded, even by his enemies. Finally, it is not from any *pecuniary advantages* that are ordinarily attached to the profeffion of arms; for foldiers are generally poor, though part of their bufinefs be to plunder.

Indeed, I can fee but one reafon in nature, why the principle of honor fhould be felected from all human incentives, and relied on for the fupport of the military fyftem: it is becaufe it was *convenient for the governing power*; that power being in the hands of a fmall part of the community whofe bufinefs was to fupport it by impofition. No

prin-

principle of a permanent nature, whofe objeſt is unequivocal, and whofe flighteft deviations are perceptible, would have anfwered the purpofe. Juſtice, for inftance, is a principle of common ufe, of which every man can difcern the application. Should the prince fay it was *juſt*, to commence an unprovoked war with his weak neighbours and plunder their country, the falfhood would be too glaring; all men would judge for themfelves, and give him the lie; and no man would follow his ftandard, unlefs bribed by his avarice. But honor is of another nature; it is what we all can feel, but no one can define; it is therefore whatever the prince may choofe to name it; and fo powerful is its operation, that all the ufeful fentiments of life lofe their effeſt; morality is not only banifhed from political cabinets, but generally and profeffionally from the bofoms of men who purfue honor in the profeffion of arms.

It is common for a king, who wifhes to make a thing fafhionable, to practife it himfelf; and in this he is fure of general imitation and fuccefs. As this device is extremely natural, and as the exiftence

iftence of wars is abfolutely neceffary to the exiftence of kings; to give a fafhion to the trade
muft have been a confiderable motive to the ancient kings, for expofing themfelves fo much as
they ufually did in battle. They faid, *Let human
flaughter be honorable*, and honorable it was.

Hence it is, that warriors have been termed heroes; and the eulogy of heroes has been the con-
ftant bufinefs of hiftorians and poets, from the
days of Nimrod down to the prefent century.
Homer, for his aftonifhing variety, animation, and
fublimity, has not a warmer admirer than myfelf;
he has been for three thoufand years, like a reign-
ing fovereign, applauded as a matter of courfe,
whether from love or fear; for no man with fafety
to his own character can refufe to join the chorus
of his praife. I never can exprefs (and his other
admirers have not done it for me) the pleafure I
receive from his poems; but in a view of philanthropy, I confider his exiftence as having been a
ferious misfortune to the human race. He has
given to military life a charm which few men can
refift, a fplendor which envelopes the fcenes of carnage

nage in a cloud of glory, which dazzles the eyes of every beholder, fteals from us our natural fenfibilities in exchange for the artificial, debafes men to brutes under the pretext of exalting them to gods, and obliterates with the fame irrefiftible ftroke the moral duties of life and the true policy of nations. Alexander * is not the only human monfter that has been formed after the model. of Achilles; nor Perfia and Egypt the only countries depopulated for no other reafon than the defire of rivalling predeceffors in military fame.

Another device of princes, to render honorable the profeffion of arms, was to make it enviable, by depriving the loweft orders of fociety of the power

* It is not unworthy of remark, that Ariftotle was the tutor of Alexander, and the moft fplendid editor and commentator of Homer. As we muft judge an author by his works, it is but fair to take into view the *whole* of his works. Confidered therefore as a political fchool-mafter to the world, the forming of his pupil and the illuftrating of his poet are the greateft fruits of the induftry of that philofopher, and have had much more influence on the affairs of nations, than his treatife that bears the name of *politics.*

of becoming foldiers. Excluding the helots of all nations from any part in the glory of butchering their fellow-creatures, has had the fame effect as in Sparta,—it has ennobled the trade; and this is the true feudal eftimation, in which this trade has defcended to us from our Gothic anceftors.

At the fame time that the feudal fyftem was furnifhing Europe with a numerous body of nobleffe, it became neceffary; for various purpofes of defpotifm, that they fhould be prevented from mingling with the common mafs of fociety, that they fhould be held together by what they call *l'efprit de corps*, or the corporation fpirit, and be furnifhed with occupations which fhould leave them nothing in common with their fellow men. Thefe occupations were offered by the church and the army; and as the former was permanent, it was thought expedient to give permanency to the latter. Thus the military fyftem has created the nobleffe, and the nobleffe the military fyftem. They are mutually neceffary to each other's exiftence,—concurrent and reciprocal caufes and effects, generating and generated, perpetuating each other by inter-

changeable

changeable wants, and both indifpenfable to the governing power.

Thofe perfons therefore who undertake to defend the nobleffe as a neceffary order in the great community of men, ought to be apprifed of the extent of their undertaking. They muft, in the firft place, defend *ftanding armies*, and that too upon principles; not of national prudence, as relative to the circumftances of neighbours, but of internal neceffity, as relative only to the organization of fociety. They muft at the fame time extend their arguments to the increafe of thofe armies; for they infallibly muft increafe to a degree beyond our ordinary calculation, or they will not anfwer the purpofe; both becaufe the number of the nobleffe, or " the men of the fword" (as they are properly ftyled by their fiiend Burke) is conftantly augmenting, and becaufe the influence of the church is on the decline. As the light of philofophy illuminates the world, it fhines in upon the fecrets of government; and it is neceffary to make the blind as broad as the window, or the paffengers will fee what is doing in the cabinet.

The

The means of impofition muft be increafed in the army, in proportion as they are loft in the church.

Secondly, they muft vindicate *war*, not merely as an occurrence of fatality, and juftifiable on the defenfive; but as a thing of choice, as being the moft nutritious aliment of that kind of government which requires privileged orders and an army: for it is no great figure of fpeech, to fay that the nobility of Europe are always fed upon human gore. They originated in war, they live by war, and without war it would be impoffible to keep them from ftarving. Or, to drop the figure entirely, if mankind were left to the peaceable purfuit of induftry, the titled orders would lofe their diftinctions, mingle with fociety, and become reafonable creatures.

Thirdly, they muft defend the *honor* of the occupation which is allotted to the nobleffe. For the age is becoming extremely fceptical on this fubject; there are heretics in the world (Mr. Burke calls them atheifts) who affect to difbelieve that men were made exprefly for the purpofe of cutting

each

each other's throats; and who fay that it is not the higheft honor that a man can arrive at, to fell himfelf to another man for life at a certain daily price, and to hold himfelf in readinefs, night and day, to kill individuals or nations, at home or abroad, without ever enquiring the caufe. Thefe men fay, that it is no compliment to the judgment or humanity of a man, to lead fuch a life; and they do not fee why a nobleman fhould not poffefs thefe qualities as well as other people.

Fourthly, they muft prove that all occupations which tend to *life*, and not to *death*, are difhonorable and infamous. Agriculture, commerce, every method of augmenting the means of fubfiftence, and raifing men from the favage flate, muft be held ignoble; or elfe men of honor will forget themfelves fo far as to engage in them; and then, farewell to diftinctions. The national affembly may then create orders as faft as it has ever uncreated them; it is impoffible for Nobility to exift, in France, or in any other country, unlefs the above articles are firmly defended by arguments, and fixed in the minds of mankind.

It

It seems difficult for a man of reflection to write one page on the subject of government, without meeting with some old established maxims, which are not only false, but which are precisely the reverse of truth. Of this fort is the opinion, That inevitable wars in modern times have given occasion to the present military system, and that standing armies are the best means of preventing wars. This is what the people of Europe are commanded to believe. With all due deference, however, to their commanders, I would propose a contrary belief, which I will venture to lay down as the true state of the fact: *That the present military system has been the cause of the wars of modern times, and that standing armies are the best, if not the only, means of* PROMOTING *wars.* This position has at least one advantage over those that are commonly established by governments, that it is believed by him who proposes it to the assent of others. Men who cannot command the power of the state, ought to enforce their doctrines by the power of Reason, and to risk on the sea of opinion nothing more than what she will take under her convoy.

To apply this maxim to the cafe now before us; let us afk, *What is war?* and on what propenfity in human nature does it reft? For it is to MAN that we are to trace thefe queftions, and not to *princes;* we muft drive them up to *principle,* and not ftop fhort at *precedent;* and endeavour to ufe our fenfe, inftead of parading our learning. Among individual men, or favages acting in a defultory manner, antecedent to the formation of great focieties, there may be many caufes of quarrels and affaffinations; fuch as love, jealoufy, rapine, or the revenge of private injuries. But thefe do not amount to the idea of war. War fuppofes a vaft affociation of men engaged in one caufe, actuated by one fpirit, and carrying on a bloody conteft with another affociation in a fimilar predicament. Few of the motives which actuate private men can apply at once to fuch a multitude, the greateft part of which muft be perfonal ftrangers to each other. Indeed, where the motives are clearly explained and well underftood by the community at large, fo as to be really felt by the people, there is but one of the ordinary caufes above mentioned which can actuate fuch a body; it is *rapine,* or the

hope

hope of enriching themfelves by plunder. There can be then but two circumftances under which a nation will commence an offenfive war: either the people at large muft be thoroughly convinced that they fhall be perfonally rewarded not only with conqueft, but with a vaft fhare of wealth from the conquered nation, or elfe they muft be duped into the war by thofe who hold the reins of government. All motives for national offences are reduced to thefe two, and there can be no more. The fubject, like moft others, becomes extremely fimple, the moment it is confidered.

And how many of the wars of mankind originate in the firft of thefe motives? Among civilized nations, none. A people confiderably numerous, approaching towards ideas of fober policy, and beginning to tafte the fruits of induftry, require but little experience to convince themfelves of the following truths,—that no benefit can be derived to the great body of individuals from conqueft, though it were certain—that this event is always doubtful, and the decifion to be dreaded,—that nine tenths of the loffes in all wars are a *clear* lofs to both

parties,

parties, being funk in expences,—that the remaining tenth neceffarily comes into the hands of the
principal managers, and produces a real misfortune even to the victorious party, by giving them
mafters at home, inftead of riches from abroad.

The pitiful idea of feafting ourfelves on a com-
parifon of fuffering, and balancing our own loffes
by thofe of the enemy, is a ftratagem of government, a calculation of cabinet arithmetic. Individuals reafon not in this manner. A diftreffed
mother in England, reduced from a full to a fcanty
diet, and bewailing the lofs of her fon, receives no
confolation from being told of a woman in France,
whofe fon fell in the fame battle, and that the taxes
are equally increafed in both countries by the fame
war. But kings, and minifters, and generals, and
hiftorians proclaim, as a glorious conteft, every
war which appears to have been as fatal to the
enemy as to their own party, though one half of
each nation are flaughtered in the field, and the
other half reduced to flavery. This is one of the
bare-faced impofitions with which mankind are perpetually infulted, and which call upon us, in the

name

name of humanity, to purfue this enquiry into the caufes of war.

The hiftory of ancient Rome, from beginning to end, under all its kings, confuls and emperors, furnifhes not a fingle inftance, after the conqueft of the Sabines, of what may properly be called a *popular* offenfive war ; I mean a war that would have been undertaken by the people, had they enjoyed a free government, fo organized as to have enabled them to deliberate before they acted, and to fuffer nothing to be carried into execution but the national will.

The fame may be faid of modern Europe, after a correfponding period in the progrefs of nations ; which period fhould be placed at the very commencement of civilization. Perhaps after the fettlement of the Saracens in Spain, the Lombards in Italy, the Franks in Gaul, and the Saxons in England, we fhould have heard no more of offenfive operations, had they depended on the uninfluenced wifhes of the people. For we are not to

regard

regard as *offensive* the struggles of a nation for the recovery of liberty.

What an inconceivable mass of slaughter are we then to place to the other account; to dark, unequal government! to the magical powers possessed by a few men of blinding the eyes of the community, and leading the people to destruction by those who are called their fathers and their friends! These operations could not be carried on, for a long time together, in ages tolerably enlightened, without a permanent resource. As long as the military conditions of feudal tenures remained in full vigor, they were sure to furnish the means of destruction to follow the will of the sovereign; but as the asperities of this system softened away by degrees, it seems that governments were threatened with the necessity of applying to the people at large for voluntary enlistments, and contributions in money; on which application the purpose must be declared. This would be too direct an appeal to the consciences of men on a question of offensive war, and was, if possible, to be avoided. For even the power of the church, where there was no

question

queſtion of hereſy, could not be always relied on, to ſtimulate the people to a quarrel with their neigh-bours of the ſame faith; and ſtill leſs was it ſure of inducing them to part with their money. The expedient therefore of ſtanding armies became ne-ceſſary; and perhaps rather on account of the money than the men. Thus money is required to levy armies, and armies to levy money; and foreign wars are introduced as the pretended occa-ſion for both.

One general character will apply to much the greater part of the wars of modern times,———— they are *political*, and not *vindictive*. This alone is ſufficient to account for their real origin. They are wars of agreement *, rather than of diſſention;

* Whenever the real ſecret hiſtory of the Engliſh and Spa-niſh armaments of 1790 ſhall be publiſhed to the world, though it may not furniſh new arguments to men of reflection for dif-truſting political cabinets, it may at leaſt increaſe the number of ſuch men. But this cannot be done with ſafety during the lives of ſome of the principal actors in that aſtoniſhing piece of audacity. I am convinced that the perſon who at this moment ſhould do it, would not ſurvive the publication ſo long as pope Ganganelli did the ſuppreſſion of the Jeſuits.

and

and the conqueſt is taxes, and not territory. To carry on this buſineſs, it is neceſſary not only to keep up the military ſpirit of the nobleſſe by titles and penſions, and to keep in pay a vaſt number of troops, who know no other God but their king; who loſe all ideas of themſelves, in contemplating their officers; and who forget the duties of a man, to practiſe thoſe of a ſoldier,—this is but half the operation: an eſſential part of the military ſyſtem is to diſarm the people, to hold all the functions of war, as well the arm that executes, as the will that declares it, equally above their reach. This part of the ſyſtem has a double effect, it palſies the hand and brutalizes the mind: an habitual diſuſe of phyſical forces totally deſtroys the moral; and men loſe at once the power of protecting themſelves, and of diſcerning the cauſe of their oppreſſion,

It is almoſt uſeleſs to mention the concluſions which every rational mind muſt draw from theſe conſiderations. But though they are too obvious to be miſtaken, they are ſtill too important to be paſſed over in ſilence; for we ſeem to be arrived

at

at that epoch in human affairs, when " all ufeful ideas, and truths the moft neceffary to the happinefs of mankind, are no longer exclufively deftined to adorn the pages of a book *." Nations, wearied out with impofture, begin to provide for the fafety of man, inftead of purfuing his deftruction.

I will mention as one conclufion, which bids fair to be a practical one, that the way to prevent wars is not merely to change the military fyftem; for that, like the' church, is a neceffary part of the governments as they now ftand, and of fociety as now organized: but the *principle of government* muft be completely changed; and the confequence of this will be fuch a total renovation of fociety, as to banifh ftanding armies, overturn the military fyftem, and exclude the poffibility of war.

Only admit the original, unalterable truth, *that all men are equal in their rights*, and the foundation of every thing is laid; to build the fuperftructure requires no effort but that of natural deduction.

* L'Affemblée nationale.

The

The firſt neceſſary deduction will be, that the peo-ple will form an equal repreſentative government; in which it will be impoſſible for *orders* or *privi-leges* to exiſt for a moment; and conſequently the firſt materials for ſtanding armies will be converted into peaceable members of the ſtate. Another deduction follows, That the people will be univer-ſally armed: they will aſſume thoſe weapons for ſecurity, which the art of war has invented for de-ſtruction. You will then have removed the *neceſ-ſity* of a ſtanding army by the organization of the legiſlature, and the *poſſibility* of it by the arrange-ment of the militia; for it is as impoſſible for an armed ſoldiery to exiſt in an armed nation, as for a nobility to exiſt under an equal government.

It is curious to remark how ill we reaſon on human nature, from being accuſtomed to view it under the diſguiſe which the unequal governments of the world have always impoſed upon it. During the American war, and eſpecially towards its cloſe, General Waſhington might be ſaid to poſſeſs the hearts of all the Americans. His recommendation was law, and he was able to command the whole

power

power of that people for any purpofe of defence. The philofophers of Europe confidered this as a dangerous crifis to the caufe of freedom. They *knew*, from the example of Cæfar and Sylla and Marius and Alcibiades and Pericles and Cromwell, that Wafhington would never lay down his arms, till he had given his country a mafter. But after he did lay them down, then came the miracle,—his virtue was cried up to be more than human; and it is by this miracle of virtue in him, that the Americans are fuppofed to enjoy their liberty at this day.

I believe the virtue of that great man to be equal to the higheft human virtue that has ever yet been known; but to an American eye no extraordinary portion of it could appear in that tranfaction. It would have been impoffible for the general or the army to have continued in the field after the enemy left it; for the fodiers were all *citizens*; and if it had been otherwife, their numbers were not the hundredth part of the citizens at large, who were all *foldiers*. To fay that he was wife in difcerning the impoffibility of fuccefs in an

attempt to imitate the great heroes above-mentioned, is to give him only the fame merit for fa-
gacity which is common to every other perfon
who knows that country, or who has well confidered the effects of equal liberty.

Though infinite praife is due to the conftituting
affembly of France for the temperate refolution
and manly firmnefs which maik their operations
in general; yet it muft be confeffed that fome of
their reforms bear the marks of too timorous a
hand. Preferving an hereditary king with a tremendous accumulation of powers, and providing
an unneceffary number of priefts, to be paid from
the national purfe, and furnifhed with the means of
rebuilding the half-deftroyed ruins of the hierarchy,
are circumftances to be pardoned for reafons which
I have already hinted. But the enormous military
force, which they have decreed fhall remain as a
permanent eftablifhment, appears to me not only
unneceffary, and even dangerous to liberty, but
totally and directly fubverfive of the end they had
in-view. Their objects were the fecurity of the
frontiers and the tranquillity of the ftate; the re-
verfe

verfe of this will be the effect,—not perhaps that this army will be turned againft the people, or involve the ftate in offenfive wars. On the contrary, fuppofe that it fimply and faithfully defends the frontiers and protects the people; this defence and this protection are the evils of which I complain. They tend to weaken the nation, by deadening the fpirit of the people, and teaching them to look up to others for protection, inftead of depending on their own invincible arm. A people that legiflate for themfelves ought to be in the habit of protecting themfelves; or they will lofe the fpirit of both. A knowledge of their own *ftrength* preferves a temperance in their own *wifdom*, and the performance of their *duties* gives a value to their *rights*.

This is likewife the way to increafe the folid domeftic force of a nation, to a degree far beyond any ideas we form of a ftanding army; and at the fame time to annihilate its capacity as well as inclination for foreign aggreffive hoftilities. The true guarantee of perpetual tranquillity at home and abroad, in fuch a cafe, would arife from this

truth,

truth, which would paſs into an incontrovertible maxim, that offenſive operations would be impoſſible, and defenſive ones infallible.

This is undoubtedly the true and only ſecret of exterminating wars from the face of the earth; and it muſt afford no ſmall degree of conſolation to every friend of humanity, to find this unſpeakable bleſſing reſulting from that equal mode of government, which alone ſecures every other enjoyment for which mankind unite their intereſts in ſociety. Politicians, and even ſometimes honeſt men, are accuſtomed to ſpeak of war as an uncontrolable event, falling on the human race like a concuſſion of the elements,—a ſcourge which admits no remedy; but for which we muſt wait with trembling preparation, as for an epidemical diſeaſe, whoſe force we may hope to lighten, but can never avoid. They ſay that mankind are wicked and rapacious, and " it muſt be that offences will come." This reaſoning applies to individuals, and to countries when governed by individuals; but not to nations deliberately ſpeaking a national voice. I hope I ſhall not be underſtood to mean,

that

that the nature of man is totally changed by living in a free republic. I allow that it is still *interested* men and *paffionate* men, that direct the affairs of the world. But in national affemblies, paffion is loft in deliberation, and intereft balances intereft; till the good of the whole community combines the general will. Here then is a great moral entity, acting ftill from interefted motives; but whofe intereft it never can be, in any poffible combination of circumftances, to commence an offenfive war.

There is another confideration, from which we may argue the total extinction of wars, as a neceffary confequence of eftablifhing governments on the reprefentative wifdom of the people. We are all fenfible that fuperftition is a blemifh of human nature, by no means confined to fubjects connected with religion. Political fuperftition is almoft as ftrong as religious; and it is quite as univerfally ufed as an inftrument of tyranny. To enumerate the variety of ways in which this inftrument operates on the mind, would be more difficult, than to form a general idea of the refult of

its

its operations. In monarchies, it induces men to fpill their blood for a particular family, or for a particular branch of that family, who happens to have been born firſt, or laſt, or to have been taught to repeat a certain creed, in preference to other creeds. But the effect which I am going chiefly to notice, is that which refpects the territorial boundaries of a government. For a man in Portugal or Spain to prefer belonging to one of thoſe nations rather than the other, is as much a fuperſtition, as to prefer the houſe of Braganza to that of Bourbon, or Mary the fecond of England, to her brother. All theſe fubjects of preference ſtand upon the fame footing as the turban and the hat, the crofs and the crefcent, or the lilly and the rofe.

The boundaries of nations have been fixed for the accommodation of the *government*, without the leaſt regard to the convenience of the people. Kings and miniſters, who make a profitable trade of governing, are intereſted in extending the limits of their dominion as far as poſſible. They have a property in the people, and in the territory that

H   they

they cover. The country and its inhabitants are to them a farm flocked with sheep. When they call up these sheep to be sheared, they teach them to know their names, to follow their master, and avoid a stranger. By this unaccountable impofition it is, that men are led from one extravagant folly to another,—to adore their king, to boast of their nation, and to wish for conquest,—circumstances equally ridiculous in themselves, and equally incompatible with that rational estimation of things, which arifes from the science of liberty.

In America it is not fo. Among the several states, the governments are all equal in their force, and the people are all equal in their rights. Were it possible for one state to conquer another state, without any expence of money, or of time, or of blood,—neither of the states, nor a single individual in either of them, would be richer or poorer for the event. The people would all be upon their own lands, and engaged in their own occupations, as before; and whether the territory on which they live were called New York or Massachusetts, is a matter of total indifference, about which

which they have no fuperftition. For the people belong not to the government, but the government belongs to the people.

Since the independence of thofe ftates, many territorial difputes have been fettled, which had rifen from the interference of their ancient charters. The interference of charters is a kind of policy which, I fuppofe, every mother country obferves towards her colonies, in order to give them a fubject of contention; that fhe may have the opportunity of keeping all parties quiet by the parental blefling of a ftanding army. But on the banifhment of foreign controul, and all ideas of European policy, the enjoyment of equal liberty has taught the Americans the fecret of fettling thefe difputes, with as much calmnefs as they have formed their conftitutions. It is found, that queftions about the boundaries between free ftates are not matters of intereft, but merely of form and convenience. And though thefe queftions may involve a tract of country equal to an European kingdom, it alters not the cafe; they are fettled as merchants fettle the courfe of exchange between

two

two commercial cities. Several inftances have occurred, fince the revolution, of deciding in a few days, by amicable arbitration, territorial difputes, which determine the jurifdiction of larger and richer tracts of country, than have formed the objects of all the wars of the two laft centuries between France and Germany.

It is needlefs to fpend any time in applying this idea to the circumftances of all countries, where the government fhould be freely and habitually in the hands of the people. It would apply to all Europe; and will apply to it, as foon as a revolution fhall take place in the principle of government. For fuch a revolution cannot ftop fhort of fixing the power of the ftate on the bafis allotted by nature, the unalienable rights of man; which are the fame in all countries. It will eradicate the fuperftitions about territorial jurifdiction; and this confideration muft promife an additional fecurity againft the poffibility of war.

CHAP.

CHAP. IV.

The Administration of Justice.

IT would be a curious speculation, and perhaps as useful as curious, to consider how far the moral nature of man is affected by the organization of society; and to what degree his predominant qualities depend on the nature of the government under which he lives. The adage, *That men are every where the same,* though not wholly false, would doubtless be found to be true only in a limited sense. I love to indulge the belief, that it is true so far as to ensure permanency to institutions that are good; but not so far as to discourage us from attempting to reform those that are bad. To consider it as true in an unlimited sense, would be to serve the purposes of despotism; for

H 3

which

which this, like a thoufand other maxims, has been invented and employed. It would teach us to fit down with a gloomy fatisfaction on the ftate of human affairs, to pronounce the race of man emphatically " fated to be curft," a community of felf-tormentors and mutual affaffins, bound down by the irrefiftible deftiny of their nature to be robbed of their reafon by priefts, and plundered of their property by kings. It would teach us to join with Soame Jenyns, and furnifh new weapons to the oppreffors, by our manner of pitying the misfortunes of the oppreffed.

In confirmation of this adage, and as an apology for the exifting defpotifms, it is faid, That all men are by nature tyrants, and will exercife their tyrannies, whenever they find opportunity. Allowing this affertion to be true, it is furely cited by the wrong party. It is an apology for equal, and not for unequal governments ; and the weapon belongs to thofe who contend for the republican principle. If government be founded on the vices of mankind, its bufinefs is to reftrain thofe vices in all, rather than to fofter them in a few. The difpofi-

tion

tion to tyrannize is effectually reftrained under the exercife of the equality of rights; while it is not only rewarded in the few, but invigorated in the many, under all other forms of the focial connexion. But it is almoft impoffible to decide, among moral propenfities, which of them belong to nature, and which are the offspring of habit; how many of our vices are chargeable on the permanent qualities of man, and how many refult from the mutable energies of ftate.

If it be in the power of a bad government to render men worfe than nature has made them, why fhould we fay it is not in the power of a good one to render them better ? and if the latter be capable of producing this effect in any perceivable degree, where fhall we limit the progrefs of human wifdom and the force of its inftitutions, in ameliorating not only the focial condition, but the controlling principles of man ?

Among the component parts of government, that, whofe operation is the moft direct on the moral habits of life, is the Adminiftration of Juftice.

In

In this every perfon has a peculiar ifolated intereft, which is almoft detached from the common fym-'pathies of fociety. It is this which operates with a fingular concentrated energy, collecting the whole force of the ftate from the community at large, and bringing it to act upon a fingle individual, affecting his life, reputation or property; fo that the governing power may fay with peculiar propriety to the minifter of juftice, *divide et impera*; for, in cafe of oppreffion, the victim's cries will be too feeble to excite oppofition; his caufe having nothing in common with that of the citizens at large. If therefore we would obtain an idea of the condition of men on any given portion of the earth, we muft pay a particular attention to their judiciary fyftem, not in its form and theory, but in its fpirit and practice. It may be faid in general of this part of the civil polity of a nation, that as it is a ftream flowing from the common fountain of the government, and muft be tinged with whatever impurities are found in the fource from whence it defcends, the only hope of cleanfing the ftream is by purifying the fountain.

If

If I were able to give an energetic fketch of the office and dignity of a rational fyftem of jurif-prudence, defcribe the full extent of its effects on the happinefs of men, and then exhibit the per-verfions and corruptions attendant on this bu-finefs in moft of the governments of Europe, it would furnifh one of the moft powerful argu-ments in favor of a general revolution, and afford no fmall confolation to thofe perfons who look forward with certainty to fuch an event. But my plan embraces too many fub-jects, to be particular on any; all that I can promife myfelf, is to feize the rough features of fyftems, and mark the moral attitudes of man as placed in the neceffary pofture to fupport them.

It is generally underftood that the object of government, in this part of its adminiftration, is merely to *reftrain* the vices of men. But there is another object prior to this; an office more facred, and equally indifpenfable, is to *prevent* their vices,—to correct them in their origin, or eradicate them totally from the

adolefcent

adolefcent mind. The latter is performed by inftruction, the former by coertion; the one is the tender duty of a father, the other, the un-relenting drudgery of a mafter; but both are the bufinefs of government, and ought to be made concurrent branches of the fyftem of jurif-prudence.

The abfurd and abominable doctrine, *that private vices are public benefits*, it is hoped, will be blotted from the memory of man, expunged from the catalogue of human follies, with the fyftems of governments which gave it birth. The ground of this infulting doctrine is, that advantage may be taken of the extravagant foibles of individuals to increafe the revenues of the ftate; as if the chief end of fociety were, to fteal money for the government's purfe! to be fquandered by the governors, to render them more infolent in their opprefficons! It is humi-liating, to anfwer fuch arguments as thefe; where we muft lay open the moft degrading re-treats of proftituted logic, to difcover the pofi-tions on which they are founded. But *Orders* and

Pri-

Privileges will lead to any thing : once teach a man, that *some are born to command and others to be commanded*; and after that, there is no camel too big for him to fwallow.

This idea of the objects to be kept in view by the fyftem of Juftice, involving in it the bufinefs of prevention as well as of reftriction, leads us to fome obfervations on the particular fubject of criminal jurifprudence. Every fociety, confidered in itfelf as a moral and phyfical entity, has the undoubted faculty of felf-prefervation. It is an independent being ; and, towards other beings in like circumftances of independence, it has a right to ufe this faculty of defending itfelf, without previous notice to the party ; or without the obfervance of any duty, but that of abftaining from offenfive operations. But when it acts towards the members of its own family, towards thofe dependent and defencelefs beings that make part of itfelf, the *right* of coercion is preceded by the *duty* of inftruction. It may be fafely pronounced, *that a ftate has no right to punifh a man, to whom it has given no previous in-*
ftruction;

ſtruction; and confequently, any perſon has a right to do any action, unleſs he has been informed that it has an evil tendency. It is true, that as relative to particular cafes, the having given this information is a thing that the fociety muſt fometimes *preſume*, and is not always obliged to *prove*. But thefe cafes are rare, and ought never to form a general rule. This prefumption has however paffed into a general rule, and is adopted as univerfal practice. With what juſtice or propriety it is fo adopted, a very little reflection will enable us to decide.

The great outlines of morality are extremely fimple and eafy to be underſtood; they may be faid to be written on the heart of a man antecedent to his aſſociating with his fellow-creatures. As a felf-dependent being he is felf-inſtructed; and as long as he ſhould remain a fimple child of *nature*, he would receive from nature all the leſſons neceſſary to his condition. He would be a complete moral agent; and ſhould he violate the rights of another independent man like himſelf, he would ſin againſt fufficient

ficient light, to merit any punifhment that the
offended party might inflict upon him. But
fociety opens upon us a new field of contemplation; it furnifhes man with another clafs of
rights, .and impofes upon him an additional
fyftem of duties; it enlarges the fphere of his
moral agency, and makes him a kind of artificial being, propelling and propelled by new de-
pendencies, in which Nature can no longer ferve
him as a guide. Being removed from her rudi-
mental fchool, and entered in the college of Society, he is called to encounter problems which
the elementary tables of his heart will not always
enable him to folve. Society then ought to be
confiftent with herfelf in her own inftitutions;
if fhe fketches the lines of his duty with a vari-
able pencil, too flight for his natural perception,
fhe fhould lend him her optical glaffes to difcern
them; if fhe takes the ferule in one hand, fhe
is bound to ufe the fefcue with the other.

We muft obferve farther,—that though Society itfelf be a ftate of nature, as relative to
the nation at large,—though it be a ftate to
which

which mankind naturally recur to satisfy their wants and increase the sum of their happiness,—though all its laws and regulations may be perfectly reasonable, and calculated to promote the good of the whole,—yet, with regard to an individual member, his having *consented* to these laws, or even chosen to live in the society, is but a *fiction*; and a rigid discipline founded on a fiction, is surely hard upon its object. In general it may be said, that a man comes into society by birth; he neither consents nor dissents respecting his relative condition; he firsts opens his eyes on that state of human affairs in which the interests of his moral associates are infinitely complicated; with these his duties are so blended and intermingled, that nature can give him but little assistance in finding them out. His morality itself must be arbitrary; it must be varied at every moment, to comprehend some local and positive regulation; his science is to begin where that of preceding ages has ended; his alpha is their omega; and he is called upon to act by instinct what they have but learnt to do from the experience of all mankind. Natural

reason

reafon may teach me not to ftrike my neighbour without a caufe; but it will never forbid my fending a fack of wool from England, or printing the French conftitution in Spain. Thefe are pofitive prohibitions, which Nature has not written in her book; fhe has therefore never taught them to her children. The fame may be faid of all regulations that arife from the focial compact.

It is a truth, I believe, not to be called in queftion, that every man is born with an imprefcriptible claim to a portion of the elements; which portion is termed his *birth-right*. Society may vary this right, as to its form, but never can deftroy it in fubftance. She has no control over the man, till he is born; and the right being born with him, and being neceffary to his exiftence, fhe can no more annihilate the one than the other, though fhe has the power of new-modeling both. But on coming into the world, he finds that the ground which nature had promifed him is taken up,

and

and in the occupancy of others; Society has changed the form of his birth-right; the general flock of elements, from which the lives of men are to be fupported, has undergone a new modification; and his portion among the reft. He is told that he cannot claim it in its prefent form, as an independant inheritance; that he muft draw on the flock of fociety, inftead of the ftock of nature; that he is banifhed from the mother, and muft cleave to the nurfe. In this unexpected occurrence he is unprepared to act; but *knowledge* is a part of the ftock of fociety; and an indifpenfable part to be allotted in the portion of the claimant, is *inftruction* relative to the new arrangement of natural right. To withhold this inftruction therefore would be, not merely the omiffion of a duty, but the commiffion of a crime; and fociety in this cafe would fin againft the man, before the man could fin againft fociety.

I fhould hope to meet the affent of all un-prejudiced readers, in carrying this idea ftill farther. In cafes where a perfon is born of poor parents,

parents, or finds himfelf brought into the community of men without the means of fubfiftence, fociety is bound in duty to furnifh him the means. She ought not only to inftruct him in the artificial laws by which property is fecured, but in the artificial induftry by which it is obtained. She is bound, in *juftice* as well as policy, to give him fome art or trade. For the reafon of his incapacity is, that *fhe* has ufurped his birth-right; and this is reftoring it to him in another form, more convenient for both parties. The failure of fociety in this branch of her duty, is the occafion of much the greater part of the evils that call for criminal jurifprudence. The individual feels that he is robbed of his natural right; he cannot bring his procefs to reclaim it from the great community, by which he is overpowered; he therefore feels authorized in reprifal; in taking another's goods to replace his own. And it muft be confeffed, that in numberlefs inftances the conduct of fociety juftifies him in this proceeding; fhe has feized upon his property, and commenced the war againft him.

Some

Some, who perceive thefe truths, fay that it is unfafe for fociety to publifh them , but I fay it is unfafe not to publifh them. For the party from which the mifchief is expected to arife, has the knowledge of them already, and has acted upon them in all ages. It is the wife who are ignorant of thefe things, and not the foolifh. They are truths of nature; and in them the teachers of mankind are the only party that remains to be taught. It is a fubject on which the logic of indigence is much clearer than that of opulence. The latter reafons from contrivance, the former from feeling; and God has not endowed us with falfe feelings, in things that fo weightily concern our happinefs.

None can deny that the obligation is much ftronger on me, to fupport my life, than to fup-port the claim that my neighbour has to his pro-perty. Nature commands the firft, fociety the fecond:—in one I obey the laws of God, which are univerfal and eternal; in the other, the laws.of man, which are local and temporary.

It

It has been the folly of all old governments, to begin every thing at the wrong end, and to erect their inftitutions on an inverfion of principle. This is more fadly the cafe in their fyftems of jurifprudence, than is commonly imagined. *Compelling* juftice is always miftaken for *rendering* juftice. But this important branch of adminiftration confifts not merely in compelling men to be juft to each other, and individuals to fociety,—this is not the whole, nor is it the principal part, nor even the beginning, of the operation. The fource of power is faid to be the fource of juftice; but it does not anfwer this defcription, as long as it contents itfelf with *compulfion.* Juftice muft begin by flowing from its fource; and the firft as well as the moft important object is, to open its channels from fociety to all the individual members. This part of the adminiftration being well devifed and diligently executed, the other parts would leffen away by degrees to matters of inferior confideration.

It is an undoubted truth, that our duty is inſeparably connected with our happineſs. And why ſhould we deſpair of convincing every member of ſociety of a truth ſo important for him to know? Should any perſon object, by ſaying, that nothing like this has ever yet been done; I anſwer, that nothing like this has ever yet been tried. Society has hitherto been curſt with governments, whoſe exiſtence depended on the extinction of truth. Every moral light has been ſmothered under the buſhel of perpetual impoſition; from whence it emits but faint and glimmering rays, always inſufficient to form any luminous ſyſtem on any of the civil concerns of men. But theſe covers are crumbling to the duſt, with the governments which they ſupport; and the probability becomes more apparent, the more it is conſidered, that ſociety is capable of curing all the evils to which it has given birth.

It ſeems that men, to diminiſh the phyſical evils that ſurround them, connect themſelves in ſociety; and from this connection their moral evils arife. But the *immediate* occafion of the moral evils is nothing more than the *remainder* of the phyfical that ftill exift even under the regulations that fociety makes to banifh them. The direct object therefore of the government ought to be, to deftroy as far as poffible the remaining quantity of phyfical evils; and the moral would fo far follow their deftruction. But the miftake that is always made on this fubject is, that governments, inftead of laying the ax at the root of the tree, aim their ftrokes at the branches; they attack the moral evils *directly* by vindictive juftice, inftead of removing the phyfical by diftributive juftice.

There are two diftinct kinds of phyfical evils; one arifes from want, or the apprehenfion of want; the other from bodily difeafe. The former feems capable of being removed by fociety; the latter is inevitable. But the latter gives no occafion to moral diforders; it being the common lot of all, we all bear our part in filence, without complaining of each other, or revenging ourfelves on the community. As it

I 3

is

is out of the power of our neighbour's goods to relieve us, we do not covet them for this purpofe. The former is the only kind from which moral evils arife; and to this the energies of government ought to be chiefly directed; efpecially that part which is called the adminiftration of juftice.

No nation is yet fo numerous, nor any country fo populous, as it is capable of becoming. Europe, taken together, would fupport at leaft five times its prefent number, even on its prefent fyftem of cultivation; and how many times this increafed population may be multiplied by new difcoveries in the infinite fcience of fubfiftence, no man will pretend to calculate. This of itfelf is fufficient to prove, that fociety at prefent has the means of rendering all its members happy in every refpect, except the removal of bodily difeafe. The common ftock of the community appears abundantly fufficient for this purpofe. By common ftock, I would not be underftood to mean the goods exclufively appropriated to individuals. Exclufive property

is

is not only confiftent with good order among men, but it feems, and perhaps really is, neceffary to the exiftence of fociety. But the common ftock of which I fpeak, confifts, firft, in *knowledge*, or the improvements which men have made in the means of acquiring a fupport; and fecondly, in the *contributions* which it is neceffary fhould be collected from individuals, and applied to the maintenance of tranquillity in the ftate. The property exclufively belonging to individuals, can only be the furpluffage remaining in their hands, after deducting what is neceffary to the real wants of fociety. Society is the firft proprietor; as fhe is the original caufe of the appropriation of wealth, and its indifpenfable guardian in the hands of the individual.

Society then is bound, in the firft place, to diftribute knowledge to every perfon according to his wants, to enable him to be ufeful and happy; fo far as to difpofe him to take an active intereft in the welfare of the ftate. *Secondly*,

where

where the faculties of the individual are naturally defective, fo that he remains unable to
provide for himfelf, fhe is bound ftill to fupport
and render him happy. It is her duty in all
cafes to induce every human creature, by rational motives, to place his happinefs in the tranquillity of the public, and in the fecurity of
individual peace and property. But *thirdly*, in
cafes where thefe precautions fhall fail of their
effect, fhe is driven indeed to the laft extremi-
ty,—fhe is to ufe the rod of correction. Thefe
inftances would doubtlefs be rare; and, if we
could fuppofe a long continuance of wife adminiftration, fuch as a well organized government
would enfure to every nation in the world, we
may almoft perfuade ourfelves to believe, that
the neceffity for punifhment would be reduced
to nothing.

Proceeding however on the fuppofition of
the exiftence of crimes, it muft ftill remain an
object of legiflative wifdom, to difcriminate between their different claffes, and apply to each
its

its proper remedy, in the quantity and mode of punishment. It is no part of my subject to enter into this enquiry, any farther than simply to observe, that it is the characteristic of arbitrary governments to be jealous of their power. And, as jealousy is, of all human passions, the most vindictive and the least rational, these governments seek the revenge of injuries in the most absurd and tremendous punishments that their fury can invent. As far as any rule can be discovered in their gradation of punishments, it appears to be this, That the severity of the penalty is in proportion to the injustice of the law. The reason of this is simple,—the laws which counteract nature the most, are the most likely to be violated.

The publication, within the last half century, of a great number of excellent treatises on the subject of penal laws, without producing the least effect, in any part of Europe, is a proof that no reform is to be expected in the general system of criminal jurisprudence, but from a

radical

radical change in the principle of government *.

A method of communicating inftruction to every member of fociety, is not difficult to difcover, and would not be expenfive in practice. The government generally eftablifhes miniflers of juftice in every part of the dominion. The firft object of thefe miniflers ought to be, to fee that every perfon is well inftructed in his duties and in his rights; that he is rendered perfectly acquainted with every law, in its true fpirit and tendency, in order that he may know the reafon of his obedience, and the manner of obtaining redrefs, in cafe he fhould deem it unjuft; that he is taught to feel the cares and interefts of an active citizen, to confider himfelf

* The compaffionate little treatife of Beccaria, *dei delitti e delle pene*, is getting to be a manual in all languages. It has already ferved as an introduction to many luminous effays on the policy and right of punifhment, in which the fpirit of enquiry is purfued much farther than that benevolent philofopher, furrounded as he is by the united fabres of feudal and ecclefiaftical tyranny, has dared to purfue it.

as a real member of the ftate, know that the government is his own, that the fociety is his friend, and that the officers of the ftate are the fervants of the people. A perfon poffeffing thefe ideas will never violate the law, unlefs it be from neceffity ; and fuch neceffity is to be prevented by means which are equally obvious.

For the purpofes of compulfive juftice, it is not enough that the laws be rendered familiar to the people; but the tribunals ought to be near at hand, eafy of accefs, and equally open to the poor as to the rich ; the means of coming at juftice fhould be cheap, expeditious and certain ; the mode of procefs fhould be fimple and perfectly intelligible to the meaneft capacity, unclouded with myfteries and unperplexed with forms. In fhort, juftice fhould familiarife itfelf as the well-known friend of every man ; and the confequence feems natural, that every man would be a friend to juftice.

After confidering what is the duty of fociety, and what *would be* the practice of a well-orga-

nized

nized government, relative to the subject of this chapter, it is almost useless to enquire, what *is* the practice of all the old governments of Europe. We may be sure beforehand, that it is directly the contrary,—that, like all other parts of the system, it is the inversion of every thing that is right and reasonable. The pyramid is every where set on the little end, and all sorts of extraneous rubbish are constantly brought to prop it up.

Unequal governments are necessarily founded in ignorance, and they must be supported by ignorance; to deviate from their principle, would be voluntary suicide. The first great object of their policy is to perpetuate that undisturbed ignorance of the people, which is the companion of poverty, the parent of crimes, and the pillar of the state.

In England, the people at large are as perfectly ignorant of the acts of parliament after they are made, as they possibly can be before. They are printed by one man only, who is

called

called the king's printer,—in the old German character, which few men can read,—and fold at a price that few can afford to pay. But left fome fcraps or comments upon them fhould come to the people through the medium of public news-papers, every fuch paper is ftamped with a heavy duty; and an act of parliament is made, to prevent men from lending their papers to each other *; fo that, not one perfon in a hundred fees a news-paper once in a year. If a man at the bottom of Yorkfhire difcovers by inftinct that a law is made, which is interefting for him to know, he has only to make a journey to London, find out the king's prin-

---

* As this work may chance to fall into the hands of fome people who never fee the acts of parliament (the fame precautions not being taken to prevent its circulation) it is out of compaffion to that clafs of readers, that I give this information. It is a duty of humanity, to fave our fellow-creatures from falling into fnares, even thofe that are fpread for them by the government. Therefore: Notice is hereby given to all perfons, to whom thefe prefents fhall come, that the penalty for letting a news-paper, within the kingdom of Great-Britain, is fifty pounds.

ter,

ter, pay a penny a page for the law, and learn the German alphabet. He is then prepared to spell out his duty.

As to the general syſtem of the laws of the land, on which all property depends, no man in the kingdom knows them, and no man pretends to know them. They are a fathomleſs abyſs, that exceeds all human faculties to found. They are ſtudied, not to be underſtood, but to be diſputed; not to give information, but to breed confuſion. The man whoſe property is depending on a ſuit at law, dares not look into the gulph that ſeparates him from the wiſhed-for deciſion; he has no confidence in himſelf, nor in reaſon, nor in juſtice; he mounts on the back of a lawyer, like one of Mr. Burke's heroes of chivalry between the wings of a griffin, and truſts the pilotage of a man, who is ſuperior to himſelf, only in the confidence which reſults from having nothing at ſtake.

To penetrate into what are called the courts of juſtice, on the continent, and expoſe the ge-

neral

neral fyftem of their adminiftration, in thofe
points which are common to moft countries in
Europe, would be to lay open an inconceivable
fcene of iniquity; it would be,

> " To pour in light on Pluto's drear abodes,
> Abhorr'd by men, and dreadful e'en to gods."

What are we to do with our fenfibility, with our
honeft inftinct of propriety,—how refrain from
exclamations of horror, while we contemplate
a fet of men, affuming the facred garb of juftice, for the uniform and well-known purpofe
of felling their decifions to the higheft bidder!
For a judge to receive a bribe, we fhould think
an indelible ftain upon his character as a *man*;
but what fhall we fay of the ftate of human nature, where it is no difgrace to him as a *judge?*
Where it is not only expected as a matter of
courfe, and practifed without difguife, but is
made almoft a neceffary part of the judiciary
fyftem?

Whether the practice of receiving bribes was
the original idea on which is founded the *vena-*

lity

lity of offices in modern governments, it is not to our purpose to enquire. But certain it is, they are concomitant ideas, and coextensive practices; and it is designed that they should be so. In France, before the revolution, the office of judge was not indeed hereditary, like that of king; but it was worse; it was held up for sale by the king, and put at auction by the minister. As a part of the king's revenue arose from the sale of justice, the government sold all the offices in that department at fixed prices; but the minister made the bargains with those who would give him most. Thus the seats of the judges became objects of speculation, open to all the world; and the man whose conscience was the best fitted to make a profitable trade of deciding causes, could afford to give the highest price, and was consequently sure to be judge.

Justice then was a commodity which necessarily gave a profit to three sets of men, before it could be purchased by the suitor; even supposing it might have flowed to him in a direct channel.

channel. But this was a thing impoffible: there were other defcriptions of men, more nume- rous, if not more greedy, than thofe of whom we have fpoken, through whofe hands it muft pafs and repafs, before it could arrive at the client, who had paid his money to the judge. Thefe men, who infefted the tribunals in all ftages of the bufinefs, were divided in France into about fix claffes. For want of the precife names in Englifh to defignate all their official diftinctions, we fhall rank the whole under the general appellation of Lawyers *. But though we here confound them together, as we often do objects at a diftance; yet they were not to be fo treated by the client. He muft addrefs them all diftinctly and refpectfully, with the fame *argumentum ad patronum*, with which he had addreffed the judge; as one or more of each

---

* To avoid any fufpicion of exaggeration, I will mention by their original names fuch of thefe claffes as occur to me. There were the *confeiller, avocat, procureur, fecretaire du juge, greffier, huiffier-prifeur, huiffier-audiencier,* with all their clerks, who muft likewife all be paid, or the caufe would ftop in any ftage of its progrefs.

claſs

clafs had a neceffary part in bringing forward
and putting backward every caufe that came
into court.

Lawyers in France ferved two important purpofes, which it is fuppofed they do not ferve
in England : they added confiderably to the revenues of the crown by the purchafe of their
places; and they covered the iniquity of the
judges under the impenetrable veil of their
own. In a caufe of ordinary confequence,
there was more writing to be done in France
than there is even in England, perhaps by a
hundred and fifty pages. The reafon of this
was, that it was more neceffary to involve the
queftion in myfteries and perplexities that fhould
be abfolutely infcrutable. For it muft never
be known, either at the time of trial or ever
after, on what point or principle the caufe was
decided. To anfwer this end, the multiplying
of the different orders of the managers, as well
as increafing the quantity of writing, had an
admirable effect; it removed the poffibility of
fixing a charge of fraud or mifmanagement on

any

any one of the great fraternity, or of difcovering,
among the formidable piles of papers and parch-
ments that enveloped the myfteries of the trial,
in what ftage the iniquity was introduced.

To call this whole fyftem of operations a folemn farce, is to give no utterance to our feelings ; to fay it is a fplendid mockery of juftice,
by which individuals are robbed of their property, is almoft to fpeak in its praife. The reflecting mind cannot reft upon it a moment,
without glancing over fociety, and bewailing
the terrible inroads made upon morals public
and private, the devaftation of principle, the
outrage upon nature, the degradation of the
laft particle of dignity by which we recognize
our own refemblance in man.

Its obvious tendency is, by its enormous expence, to bar the door of juftice againft the
poor, who in fuch countries are fure to form
the great body of mankind,—to render them
enemies to fociety, by teaching that fociety is
an enemy to them,—to ftimulate them to crimes,

both

both from their own neceffities, and from the example of their mafters,—and to fpread over the people at large an incruftation of ignorance, which, excluding all ideas of their duties and their rights, compels them to forget their relation to the human race.

Are thefe to be ranked among the circumftances, which call for a change in the governments of Europe? Or are we to join with Mr. Burke, and lament as an evil of the French revolution, " That the ancient fyftem of jurif-" prudence will no more be ftudied?" The whining of that good gentleman on this idea, is about as rational, as it would be to lament that the noble fcience of Heraldry was in danger of being forgotten; or that men had loft the myftical meaning of *Abracadabra*. This word, ferving as a charm, anfwered the fame purpofe in Medicine, as heraldry does in Honor; or the old jurifprudence, in Juftice: it rendered men fuperftitious; and confequently, immoral and unhappy.

It is fo fafhionable in Europe, efpecially among Englifhmen, to fpeak in praife of the Englifh jurifprudence, and to confider it as a model of perfection, that it may feem neceffary for a perfon to begin with an apology for offering his ideas on that fubject, if he means to deviate from the opinion fo generally eftablifhed. But, inftead of doing this, I will begin by apologizing for thofe who at this day fupport the eftablifhed opinion: Your faireft apology, Gentlemen, is, that you underftand nothing of the matter. To affign any other, would be lefs favourable to your characters as honeft men.

Exclufive of the rules by which the merits of a caufe are to be decided (and which, if they could be afcertained, would be the *law*) the mere *form* of bringing a queftion before a court is of itfelf a fcience, an art, lefs underftood, and more difficult to learn, than the conftruction and ufe of the moft complicated machine, or even the motions of the heavenly bodies. It is not enough, that the adminiftration of

juftice

juftice (which ought to be as fimple as poffible)
is fo involved in perplexity, that none but men
of profeffional fkill can pretend to underftand it,
but the profeffors are divided, as in France, into
feveral diftinct claffes ; each of which is abfolutely neceffary to lend a helping hand in every
ftep of the progrefs of a caufe. This dark mul-
tiplicity of form has not only removed the
knowledge of law from the generality of men,
but has created fuch an expence in obtaining
juftice, that very few ever make the attempt.
The courts are effectually fhut againft the great
body of the people, and juftice as much out of
their reach, as if no laws exifted *

Thofe

* The provifion made in the Englifh law, enabling a perfon
to bring his fuit *in forma pauperis*, is rather an infult than a real
advantage. Certainly, not one perfon in a hundred, who is
deprived of juftice in the ordinary courfe, would ever feek it in
this ; as, in order to be entitled to it, he muft go into court
and fwear that he has not property enough to profecute his
claim. A young tradefman, and in general every perfon who
wifhes to carry on bufinefs, or has fpirit enough to feek for
juftice, has a higher intereft in eftablifhing a credit among his

con-

Thofe who have attempted to purchafe juftice through the, neceffary forms, have never
been known to pronounce eulogies on the courts.
But their number has always been fo fmall, that,
had they uttered the anathemas that the fyftem
deferves, their feeble voice could fcarcely have
been heard. No man, whofe eyes are not blind-
ed by fees or by prejudice, can look upon the
enormous mafs of writings which accumulate in
a caufe, without reflecting with indignation on
the expence; one hundredth part of which
would have been more than fufficient for every
purpofe of obtaining juftice between the parties.
A writer who fhould give the names and, defcriptions of the various parts of a procefs, with
the expences annexed to each part, would
fcarcely gain credit, except with profeffional
men. Several hundred pounds are expended

connexions in bufinefs, than in profecuting any ordinary fuit at
law. He knows, that to expofe his own poverty, efpecially
in a commercial country, would be irretrievable ruin; it would
be a *pofitive* injury; while fitting down with the lofs of his
right, without bringing his fuit, is only a negative injury.

only

only in writing Bills, Subpœnas, Pleas, De-
murrers, Anfwers, Petitions, Orders, Motions,
Amendments, Notices, Reports, &c. in a fingle caufe, where no witnefs is called. . ;

Let us trace a few of the windings, and fee
where fome of the paths lead, which are laid
down as neceffary to obtaining a decifion in
Chancery; we fhall there find how hundreds,
and fometimes thoufands of pounds are expended in a caufe, before any defence is fet up, and
where no defence is ever intended to be fet up.
The fuitor begins his incomprehenfible operation, by ftating his claim, in what is called a
Bill, which he leaves at a certain office belonging to the court, and obtains an order, called a
fubpœna, for fummoning the defendant. This
being done, the court requires the defendant to
fend an Attorney to write his name at another
office of the court. This writing the name, is
called an *appearance*; it anfwers no poffible purpofe, but that of encreafing expences and fees
of office, for which it is a powerful engine.
For if the defendant does not comply, an ex-

pence of thousands of pounds may be made, to compel him. A *capias*, a procefs for *outlawry*, a commiffion of *rebellion*, and an order and commiffion of *fequeftration*, are purfued in their proper rotine, till' he confents to write his name.

If the plaintiff has property to go through this procefs, he may be faid to be able juft to keep his ground; and his caufe is in every re_ fpect precifely where it was at firft. If he has not fufficient property, the caufe is loft for want of fees; and he is no better than if he had never been able to have begun the fuit.

We will however fuppofe that the defendant very good-naturedly writes his name; he is then entitled to a certain delay, during which, the court informs him, he muft plead, demur, or anfwer to the bil. When this time expires, he is entitled to a farther delay of four weeks. But though he is *entitled* to this farther delay, and neither the plaintiff nor the court can re_ fufe it; ftill he muft employ a follicitor to make

a brief

a brief for counfel; and this follicitor muft attend the counfel, and give him and his clerk
their fees, for moving the court for this delay,
which cannot be refufed. The counfel muft
attend the court and make the motion; the
follicitor muft attend the court, and pay for the
order, entry and copy; and then muft caufe it
to be ferved.

At the end of this term of four weeks, the
defendant is *entitled* to a farther delay of three
weeks; which again cannot be refufed. But he
muft pay his follicitor for drawing and engroffing
a petition for that purpofe, and the petition muft
be prefented, and anfwered; for which he muft
pay; he muft alfo pay for order, entry, copy, and
fervice. At the end of thefe three weeks he is
in the fame manner *entitled* to a farther delay
of two weeks; but the fame farce muft be acted
over again, to obtain it. And a very folemn farce
it is to the parties, a very pleafant farce to the
officers of the court, and a very ridiculous farce
to every body elfe.

If,

If, during all this time, the defendant had ſtopt paying, or the ſollicitor had ſtopt writing, the ſame proceſs, which was uſed to compel his appearance, muſt have been repeated: to wit, *capias*, *outlawry*, commiſſion of *rebellion*, and *ſe-queſtration*. But we have arrived at the time when the defendant is in duty bound to anſwer to the bill; and here, if he does not anſwer, then *capias*, *outlawry*, *rebellion* and *ſequeſtration* again.

Theſe terms muſt be explained to the reader; and this is the beſt opportunity to do it. For the cauſe ſtill remaining preciſely where it was at firſt, we may ſuppoſe it ſufficiently at reſt, not to move during the explanation. A *capias* is an order, to take the man, and hold him in goal till he obeys the order of the court; whe-ther it be to write his name, or any thing elſe. The word *outlawry* explains, of itſelf, this hor-rid engine of the court. A commiſſion of *rebel-lion* is an order iſſued, after the officer with the capias has ſearched and cannot find the man, and after an outlawry has taken place. It is

directed

directed to other ·perfons, requiring them to take up the man who was guilty of rebellion in refuſing to write his name. But as the officer with the capias, before outlawry, could not find the man, the iſſuing the commiſſion of rebellion *now*, has no other meaning but *fees*. A *ſequeſtration* is taking the whole property of the defendant into the hands of the court. And when this is done, the cauſe is ſoon done alſo; for no eſtate could laſt long there. When the money is gone, the proceedings ceaſe.

But let us ſuppoſe that the defendant has complied with all orders thus far, and has put in a good and ſufficient anſwer. Let us leave out of our account all motions, petitions, decrees, orders, &c. for amending the bill, for referring to Maſters the inſufficiency of anſwers, reports upon thoſe anſwers, and farther anſwers, and exceptions to Maſters' reports, and orders and deciſions relative to them; and, inſtead of enquiring into the expence of theſe, let us go back and aſk what is the uſe of all, or of any part of this proceſs? Thirty thouſand Lawyers (this is

ſaid

faid to be the number in the kingdom) are now living on juft fuch ftuff as the procefs here defcribed ; and I call on them all, to point out the purpofe that any of it ever ferved, or ever can ferve, to their clients.

It muft be remembered, that all the proceedings thus far, were to end in three pretended objects,—to compel an appearance ; to obtain the *ufual* and *legal* time for the defendant to prepare his anfwer, and to compel.him to give his anfwer. For the *appearance,* which is the folemn appellation given to the action of writing a name, it would be an infult to the underftanding of a child, to tell him that this could be of any fervice towards forwarding juftice. Next comes the fucceffion of applications and orders, for time to anfwer the bill. The practice of the court, which is the law in this cafe, allows the defendant, firft a fhort term, and then the delay of four weeks, three weeks, and two weeks ; which in all reckonings, unlefs it be in law, make nine weeks. And if that be a reafonable
time

time, when divided into three parts, why is it
not so before it is divided? And if neither the
party, nor the court, nor any body else; has a
right to refuse that term of time, why might
not the defendant take it, without the expence
of asking three times? The remainder of the
process goes to compel the defendant to give in
an answer to the bill. And what is the importance of an answer? To solve this question, let
us consider the object of the bill, to which the
answer is required.

The bill expresses the claim of the plaintiff,
and points out the nature of the decree, which
he prays may be made in his favor against the
defendant. Notice is given to the defendant,
that such a suit is pending, and that he may
appear and show cause why the decree should
not be made. Having given this notice, it is
not only cruel, but absurd, to think of forcing
him to defend himself, whether he will or no.
One would suppose it little to the purpose, to
make the attempt. Why may not the subpœna,

which

which gives notice to the defendant, point out the day, beyond which he cannot give an answer? then, if he choofes to defend, hear him candidly; but if he refufes to come, and does not choofe to defend,—proceed in the caufe; he is willing that the decree fhould pafs. Can it be reafonable,—can it be any thing fhort of flat contradiction and nonfenfe, to compel him to appear, to compel him to afk for a delay, and to compel him to defend? Can his defence be neceffary in doing juftice to the plaintiff? And, if he will not defend himfelf, can you make him? Can any one of the whole hoft of all the profeffions of the law, fhow the leaft fhadow of ufe in all this flourifh of procefs thus far, but *fees* on the one hand, and *oppreffion* on the other?

To proceed through all the forms, to the end of a fuit in Chancery, would be to write a commentary on many volumes of practice, and would be calling the patience of the reader to a trial from which it would certainly fhrink. But

there

there are parts as much worfe than what we have defcribed, as this is worfe than common fenfe. Strip from the Adminiftration of Juftice the forms that are perfectly ufelefs and oppreffive, and counfellors will have much lefs to do; while the whole order of attornies and follicitors will fall to the ground. If the myfteries of nonfenfe were out of the way, a counfellor who was called upon to hazard his reputation on the manner of conducting his client's caufe, would no more have it prepared and brought forward by an attorney, than a man of bufinefs would hazard his fortune by doing that bufinefs through an ignorant agent, which he could more eafily do himfelf. The quantity of writing, really neceffary, in a fimple and dignified fyftem of practice, is fo fmall, as to be perhaps incredible to thofe who are acquainted only with the Englifh procefs.

I have feen the mode of conducting this bufinefs in a country, where the common law of England is the general rule of decifion, and

where

where the adjudications of Weſtminſter-hall are authorities, as much as they are in Great-Britain. But the laws of that country have ſtripped legal proceſs of its principal follies; and the conſequence is, that the whole profeſſion of attornies and follicitors has vaniſhed. The counſellor does the whole buſineſs of his client; and ſo ſimple is the operation, that a man may with eaſe commence, and carry through every ſtage, to final judgment and execution, five hundred cauſes in a year. And the whole proceedings in all theſe ſhall not afford writing enough to employ a ſingle clerk one hour in twenty-four. The proceedings and judgments in five hundred cauſes, in this country, would fill a warehouſe. And yet in that country, every allegation is neceſſary in their declaration and pleadings, which is neceſſary in Weſtminſter-hall. As they are not paid by the line, their declarations have but one Count, and in that Count there is no tautology. And ſo little is the expence of ſuits, where no more is done than is neceſſary for juſtice; that judgment, in a cauſe where there is no defence, may be obtained for

L   leſs

lefs than ten fhillings ; and every perfon employed be fully paid for his fervice *

Men

* As this may awaken the curiofity of fome of my readers, I
will give the details. Suppofe a fuit to recover money due on
Note or Bond: The writ and declaration are incorporated in
one inftrument; that is, the declaration is contained in the
writ. The fheriff is ordered to read this to the defendant, or
leave a copy at his dwelling, at leaft twelve days previous to
the fitting of the court. This writ is ufually filled up in a well-
known form, in a printed blank ; of which a man may with
eafe fill a hundred in a day. For this the court taxes one fhil-
ling and fix-pence. The fheriff, if he has no travel to the defendant, is paid fix-pence for reading the writ to him, and
delivering it to the clerk of the court. It is then the duty of
the plaintiff, or of his lawyer, (who is both counfellor and
follicitor) to attend the court on the firft day of the fitting ;
and then the parties in all caufes are called by the cryer. For
this attendance the court will tax three fhillings and four-pence
halfpenny ; and if the defendant intends to make no defence he
will not anfwer when called ; and the clerk thereupon, on the
third day after calling, if no motion is made by the defendant,
enters judgment for the plaintiff; for which he has about two
fhillings ; one fhillings more is paid for a writ of execution,
which is in form and effect a *fieri facias*, a *capias ad fatisfaciendum*,
and an *elegit* : that is, it goes againft the goods and chattels of the
debtor ; and if the fheriff cannot find thofe, he is to take the
body,

Men who are habituated to the expences in-
curred in law-fuits in England, will fcarcely be
perfuaded of the extent to which a reform
would be carried, on a general deftruction of
abufes. But let them reflect, that when law
proceedings are ftripped of every thing, but
what the nature of the fubject requires, there
is no myftery left. The rational part that remains is foon comprehended, and eafily retained
in memory. This would doubtlefs augment
the number of fuits; for it would open the
courts to vaft multitudes of people, againft
whom they are now effectually fhut. But in
proportion as it increafed the number of law-
fuits, it would diminifh the quantity of *law-
bufinefs*; and the number of lawyers would
dwindle to one tenth of what it is at prefent.
In the country above alluded to, the number
of men fupported by this profeffion is to the
whole population, as one to 4600. Reduce the
lawyers here to that proportion, and there would

body, or the land. Added to thefe cofts, there is a duty of
1s. 6d. to government. Thefe feveral charges are an ample
reward for all fervices rendered.

be

be left about three thoufand in the kingdom. It is afferted, (I know not on what ground) that the prefent number is thirty thoufand. Allowing it to be true, an army of twenty-feven thoufand lawyers, on this reform, would find fome other employment. But whether the reduction would amount to the number here fuppofed, or to half of it, is a queftion of little moment. Saving the expence of maintaining twenty or thirty thoufand men in a ufelefs occupation, and fending them to profitable bufinefs, however important the object may appear, bears no proportion to the advantage of opening the door of juftice to the people, and habituating them to an eafy and well-known method of demanding their right.

There is a ftrange idea prevalent in England, (it has had its day in America) that it is good policy to raife the expences of legal proceedings above the reach of the lower claffes of people; as it leffens the number of fuits. This kind of reafoning appears too abfurd to fupport its own weight for a moment; and it

would

would be beneath our ferious notice, were it not for the reflection, that men of fuperficial refearch are perpetually caught by it. The human mind is fitted, from its own indolence, to be dazzled by the glare of a propofition; and to receive and utter for truth, what it never gives itfelf the trouble to examine. There is no paradox among all the enormities of defpotifm, but what finds its advocates from this very circumftance. We muft not therefore fcorn to encounter an argument becaufe it is foolifh. The bufinefs of fober philofophy is often a tafk of drudgery; it muft fometimes liften to the moft incoherent clamours, which would be unworthy of its attention, did they not form a part of the general din, by which mankind are deafened and mifled.

For a man to bring into court a fuit that is manifeftly unjuft, is a crime againft the ftate; to hinder him from bringing one that is juft, is a crime of the ftate againft him. It is a poor compliment to the wifdom of a nation, to fuppofe that no method can be devifed for pre-

4

venting

venting the firft of thefe evils, without run-
ning into the laft; and the laft is ten times the
greateft of the two. The French, who appear
to have been deftined to give leffons to the
world by the wifdom of their new inftitutions,
as well as by the folly of their old, have found
the fecret of impofing a fmall fine on a vexa-
tious plaintiff; and of eftablifhing many other
regulations on this fubject, which effectually
fhut the door of the tribunal againft the op-
preffor, while it eafily opens to the feebleft cry
of the oppreffed.

They have likewife eftablifhed a method of
communicating the knowledge of the laws to
every human creature in the kingdom, however ignorant he may be in other refpects.
They are printed and pafted up on public build-
ings in every town and village, and read and
explained by the curate from the pulpit in every
parifh. It is in contemplation likewife to in-
ftitute a general fyftem of public inftruction,
on a more ufeful and extenfive plan than has
ever yet been devifed. Several enlightened philofophers

lofophers are bufied in thefe refearches; and feveral focieties are formed, whofe object is to
difcover and bring forward the beft concerted
plan for this important purpofe. In their whole
fyftem of diftributing *knowledge* and *juftice*, they
feem to be aiming at a degree of perfection
which promifes great fuccefs. With all my partiality for the inftitutions of the United States,
I fhould quote them (in comparifon to thofe
of France) with lefs confidence on the fubject of
this chapter, than of any other.

In the adminiftration of juftice, the Americans are too much attached to the Englifh forms;
which ferve to increafe the expence and to myf-
ticife the bufinefs, to a degree that is manifeftly
inconfiftent with the dignity of a true republic.
But in refpect to Public Inftruction, there are
fome circumftances which deferve to be mentioned to their praife. I am going to fpeak only
of the particular ftate with which I am beft acquainted. How many of the others are better
regulated in this refpect, and how many are
worfe, I am not accurately informed. This

6

ftate

ftate (which contains lefs than 240,000 inhabitants) is divided into about one hundred towns. Thefe are fub divided into fmall portions, called fchool-diftricts, fuitable for the fupport of fmall fchools. Each of thefe diftricts has a drawback on the ftate-treafury for a fum, which bears a proportion to the public taxes paid by the inhabitants of the diftrict, and which is about half equal to the fupport of a fchool-mafter. But this fum can be drawn only on condition, that a fchool is maintained in the diftrict.

The following remarkable confequences feem to have refulted from this provifion: There is not perhaps in that ftate, a perfon of fix years old and of common intellects, who cannot read; and very few who cannot write and caft accounts!—befides the ufeful books that are found in every family, it is computed that there are in the ftate about three hundred public libraries, which have been formed by voluntary fubfcription among the people of the diftricts and the parifhes;—till about the year 1768, which was more than one hundred and thirty years after

the

the fettlement of the ftate, no capital punifhment, as I am informed, had been inflicted
within its jurifdiction, nor any perfon convicted of a capital offence; fince that period,
very few have been convicted, and thofe few
are generally Europeans by birth and educati-
on;—there is no extreme poverty in the ftate,
and no extraordinary wealth accumulated by
individuals.

It would be abfurd to fuppofe, that Public
Inftruction is by any means carried to the perfection that it ought to be, in this or any other
ftate in the univerfe. But this experiment
proves, that good morals and equal liberty are
reciprocal caufes and effects; and that they are
both the parents of national happinefs, and of
great profperity.

All governments that lay any claim to re-
fpectability or juftice have profcribed the idea
of *ex-poft-facto laws*, or laws made after the
performance of an action, conftituting that
action a crime, and punifhing the party

for

for a thing that was innocent at the time of its being done. Such laws would be fo flagrant a violation of natural right, that in the French and feveral of the American State Conftitutions, they are folemnly interdicted in their Declarations of Rights. This profcription is likewife confidered as a fundamental article of Englifh liberty, and almoft the only one that has not been habitually violated, within the prefent century. But let us refort to reafon and juftice, and afk what is the difference between a violation of this article, and the obfervance of that tremendous maxim of jurifprudence, common to all the nations above-mentioned, *ignorantia legis neminem excufat?*

Moft of the laws of fociety are pofitive regulations, not taught by nature. Indeed, fuch only are applicable to the fubject now in queftion. For *ignorantia legis* can have reference only to laws arifing out of fociety, in which our natural feelings have no concern; and where a man is ignorant of fuch a law, he is in the fame fituation as if the law did not exift. To read

read it to him from the tribunal, where he ſtands arraigned ˙for the breach of it, is to him pre-ciſely the ſame thing as it would be to originate it at the time by the ſame tribunal, for the ex-preſs purpoſe of his condemnation: The law till then, as relative to him, is not in being. He is therefore in the ſame predicament that the ſociety in general would be, under the opera-tion of an *ex-poſt-facto* law. Hence we ought to conclude that, as it ſeems difficult for a go-vernment to diſpenſe with the maxim above-mentioned, a free people ought, in their decla-ration of rights, to provide for univerſal public inſtruction. If they neglect to do this, and mean to avoid the abſurdity of a ſelf-deſtroying policy, by adhering to a ſyſtem of juſtice which would preſerve a dignity and inſpire a confi-dence worthy the name of liberty, they ought to reject the maxim altogether; and inſert in their declaration of rights, that inſtruction alone can conſtitute a duty; and that laws can enforce no obedience, but where they are ex-plained.

It

It is truly hard and fufficiently to be regret-
ted, that any part of fociety fhould be obliged
to yield obedience to laws to which they have
not literally and perfonally confented. Such is
the ftate of things; it is neceffary that a majority fhould govern. If it be an evil to obey a
law to which we have not confented, it is at
leaft a neceffary evil; but to compel a compli-
ance with orders which are unknown, is carrying injuftice beyond the bounds of neceffity; it
is abfurd, and even impoffible. Laws in this
cafe may be avenged, but cannot be obeyed;
they may infpire terror, but can never command refpect.

F I N I S.

CPSIA information can be obtained
at www.ICGtesting.com
Printed in the USA
LVOW03s0848110817
544593LV00022B/1076/P